Assessing English Language Learners in the Content Areas

A Research-into-Practice Guide for Educators

Assessing English Language Learners in the Content Areas

A Research-into-Practice Guide for Educators

FLORIN M. MIHAI

University of Central Florida

ANN ARBOR
University of Michigan Press

ISBN-13: 978-0-472-03435-2
2013   2012   2011   2010   4   3   2   1

PREFACE ————————————————————————

FLORIN M. MIHAI

Given today's educational environment, it is impractical to talk about education without addressing the issues of accountability and measurement of educational goals and objectives. Current legislation in education, such as the No Child Left Behind Act, places a strong emphasis on accountability and Adequate Yearly Progress (AYP) for all students, including English Language Learners (ELLs). Furthermore, more and more critical educational decisions are linked to student performance on state assessments, which extend beyond reading and math to include science and social studies. However, existing structures and instruments for evaluating ELLs in core content areas such as math, science, and social science are either inadequate or just being researched or developed.

Assessing English Language Learners in the Content Areas: A Research-into-Practice Guide for Educators seeks to provide guidance to classroom teachers, staff developers, and test-item designers who want to improve ELL assessment outcomes, particularly in the areas of math, science, and social studies. The first two chapters of the book set the background for the discussion of content-area assessment for ELLs. Chapter 1, "English Language Learners in the K–12 Environment in the United States," examines several important characteristics of this rapidly growing student population, as well as critical legislation pertaining to ELLs. Chapter 2, "Assessment: Definition, Types, and General Principles," starts by providing a definition of assessment, as well as a description of various forms of assessment. It also discusses how ELL assessment is different from the assessment of English-proficient students and reviews important assessment principles educators should use in their understanding and evaluation of tests or other forms of measurement.

Chapter 3, "Large Scale Assessment in the Content Area and English Language Learners," starts with a thorough review of ELL test accommodations nationwide and continues with a review of research done on the effectiveness of these types of accommodations. Additionally, the chapter includes several useful recommendations in two areas: the design of large-scale assessments and the policies of standardized tests. Since states are likely to revise their assessment accommodations during the life of this book, updates can be found at http://pegasus.cc.ucf.edu/~fmihai/.

Chapter 4, "Classroom-Based Assessment in the Content Areas and English Language Learners," begins with emphasizing the importance of academic language proficiency in content area assessment. Then, content area teachers are provided with a solid model for assessment design and implementation, a model that successfully integrates both content area knowledge and English language proficiency in content area assessments.

Chapter 5, "Alternative Assessment Approaches in Content Area Classrooms for English Language Learners," starts with a comparison between alternative and traditional assessment in order to identify and analyze the characteristics of alternative assessment. It continues with a discussion of three popular alternative assessment instruments (performance assessment, curriculum-based measurement, and portfolios) and ends with the presentation of recommendations to increase the validity, reliability, and practicality of alternative assessments. The final chapter of the book, Chapter 6, "Essential Considerations in Assessing English Language Learners," proposes a set of three fundamental assessment practices to help content area teachers in their evaluation of their ELL progress.

It is a fact that the number of ELLs has increased at a very fast pace in the last decade. However, the resources for the evaluation of ELLs in content area classrooms have not kept pace with this massive growth in ELL population (Espinosa and Lopez, 2007). In the future, with more resources available as a result of an increased accountability regarding school and student progress, content area educators will be able to reduce the staggering number of ELLs who drop out providing they have a better understanding of assessment issues related to ELLs. For now, *Assessing English Language Learners in the Content Areas* intends to be a useful means for building that understanding.

CONTENTS

Chapter 1

English Language Learners in the K–12 Environment in the United States

---

Today's K–12 educational environment in the United States is characterized by an ever increasing diversity of its student population. Such diversity encompasses various categories of students. For example, in mainstream classrooms, other than the general student population, there are students with special educational needs. In addition to students with special needs, the general student population increasingly includes students who are not fully proficient in English. The number of students who are learning English has grown considerably in the past 10 years and is the focus of this book.

Before we start to discuss the most effective methods of assessment for English language learners, it is important to investigate the attributes of this student population. We will look at the definition of students who are learning English as an additional language, at their demographics, and at the characteristics that make them unique in the U.S. K–12 educational context. Furthermore, we will review the laws that pertain to this category of students, with a focus on the legislation that has had and will have tremendous consequences on both the large-scale and the classroom-based assessment of students who are nonnative English speakers.

English Language Learners:
Terminology, Definition, and Identification

The population of students who are learning English is extremely heterogeneous in terms of cultural and educational experiences and backgrounds. This diversity exists not only at the national level but also at the school level and, in many places, at the classroom level. In their mainstream content area classrooms, educators may have students with diverse language and cultural backgrounds who qualify as political refugees, who are recently arrived immigrants, or who were born and raised in the United States but still have difficulty communicating in English.

Terminology

This heterogeneity is reflected in the terminology and definitions attached to English language learners, or ELLs, the acronym that is widely used to identify nonnative speakers of English who are not yet fully proficient in the language. Other terms that are commonly used in the educational research and literature are *language-minority students*, *limited English proficient* (LEP) students, *English as a second language* (ESL) students, and *English for speakers of other languages* (ESOL) students. Because the term *LEP* focuses on the language deficit of nonnative English speakers, the term *ELL* is preferred instead.

Other attempts to change the focus from deficit to accomplishment have retained the acronym LEP but have assigned a different interpretation, where LEP stands for *language-enriched pupils*. Another relatively more recent term also makes an effort to be more inclusive and culturally sensitive by describing students whose language or culture differs from the dominant language or culture as *culturally and linguistically diverse* (CLD) students. According to Herrera, Murry, and Cabral (2007), CLD effectively describes students who will require differentiated assessment because of their diversity of language and culture. However, because the term *ELL* is more commonly used in educational discourse and is not perceived as being negative, this text will use the descriptor *English language learners*, or ELLs.

Definition

At the federal level, ELLs are defined by the U.S. Department of Education as national-origin minority students who are LEP. Public Law 107-110, also known as the No Child Left Behind Act (2001), defines an LEP student in its Title IX, Part A, Sec. 9101, (25) as follows:

An individual:

1. who is aged 3 through 21

2. who is enrolled or preparing to enroll in an elementary school or secondary school

3. (i) who was not born in the United States or whose native language is a language other than English

    (ii) who is a Native American or Alaska Native, or a native resident of the outlying areas

    (iii) who comes from an environment where a language other than English has had a significant impact on the individual's level of English language proficiency

    (iv) who is migratory, whose native language is a language other than English, and who comes from an environment where a language other than English is dominant

4. whose difficulties in speaking, reading, writing, or understanding the English language may be sufficient to deny the individual

    (i) the ability to meet the State's proficient level of achievement on State assessments

    (ii) the ability to successfully achieve in classrooms where the language of instructions is English

    (iii) the opportunity to participate fully in society.

At the state level, there is no uniform use of either ELL or LEP. Moreover, the definitions of these terms vary from state to state. Some states, such as Virginia, use the term LEP with the definition found in the No Child Left Behind Act, as described above (Commonwealth of Virginia Board of Education, 2002). Other states use LEP and ELL but define LEP differently from the definition found at the federal level. One example is Texas's Education Code (Chapter 29, Subchapter B), which describes LEP students as students whose primary language is not English and whose English language skills are such that the students have difficulty performing ordinary class work in English.

California used the term LEP until recently but then changed it to ELL. ELLs are described by the California Department of Education (www.cde.ca.gov) as follows:

> English learner students are those students for whom there is a report of a primary language other than English on the state-approved Home Language Survey and who, on the basis of the state approved oral language (grades kindergarten through grade twelve) assessment procedures and literacy (grades three through twelve only), have been determined to lack the clearly defined English language skills of listening comprehension, speaking, reading, and writing necessary to succeed in the school's regular instructional programs.

Does it really matter if there is no nationwide standardized definition of ELLs? Anstrom (1996) examined the advantages and disadvantages of having a definition to be used by all states. Some of the advantages are (a) a common terminology with which educational practitioners and policy makers can discuss the education and assessment of ELL students, (b) a more accurate estimation of not only the exact number of ELLs but also the distribution of ELLs nationally and statewide, with a positive effect on the distribution of resources, and (c) a less ambiguous understanding of what it means to be LEP.

The disadvantages of adopting a common definition include the following: (a) It may favor some languages or cultures over others, and (b) it may be too broad or too narrow, the classic dilemma of one size fits all. The latter will be extremely important if the states eventually agree on a definition of ELL. The definition could be a federally generated one, or it could be created by an educational agency or a political entity but universally accepted, given the extraordinary heterogeneity of the ELL population.

Identification

Similar to the variety of definitions of ELL at the state level, there is also a wide range of methods that are employed in the initial identification of ELLs. According to Macias (1998), these methods range from home language surveys to teacher interviews. Table 1 illustrates the top 10 methods of ELL identification, as identified by Macias.

At the state level, what are the methods of assessment that are used most by education agencies? If we take as an example the state of Maine, with its small, dispersed ELL population, its methods of ELL identification range

Table 1.   The Top 10 Methods of ELL Identification

ELL Identification Method	Number of States
Home language survey	46
Language proficiency test	45
Student records	40
Teacher observations	40
Parent information	38
Achievement tests	36
Informal assessment	34
Referral	34
Student grades	34
Teacher interview	31

Table 2.   Maine's Methods of ELL Identification

ELL Identification Method	Percentage of Districts Using the Method
Home language survey	86%
Student records	79%
Parent information	75%
Teacher observations	71%
Teacher interviews	51%
Informal assessments	40%
Special education teams	35%
English language proficiency tests	27%
Language assessment committee referral	24%
Student grades	24%

from home language surveys to achievement tests. Table 2 shows the most frequently used identification methods for ELLs (Maine Department of Education, 2002).

Most states use a home language survey for the identification of ELLs. This survey is designed to identify whether a language other than English is spoken at home and is generally given to the parents of potential ELL students. A typical home language survey is shown in Figure 1.

Figure 1.   Home Language Survey

Name of Student: _____

Sex: Male   Female

Date of Birth (MM/DD/YYYY): _____

School: _____

Grade: _____

Dear parent(s),

Our school needs to know if a language other than English is spoken at home. Please answer the following questions and return the form to your child's teacher. Thank you so much for all your help.

1. In what country was your child born?

2. What is the first language learned by the child?

3. What language do you most often use to speak with your child?

4. What language does the child use most often at home?

5. What language is spoken most frequently by all your family members at home?

6. What language does the child use most often with friends outside the home?

7. When did your child first enter school in the United States? In what city?

8. Has your child ever been in a bilingual or English as a second language (ESL) program?

_____   _____
Parent/Guardian Signature   Date

It is important to note that schools should not and do not rely solely on the answers provided on the home language surveys, in spite of their common use as a means of identifying ELLs. Many parents of ELLs are reluctant to place their students in language programs for limited English proficient students and prefer a more "sink or swim" approach to language learning. This approach involves no ESL or other language support intervention, and it is a violation of Title VI of the Civil Rights Act of 1964 to place an ELL student in a submersion situation (Maine Department of Education, 2002). Because ELLs must learn language and content at the same time, such an approach could potentially be very detrimental, not only to the development of academic knowledge but also to the English language proficiency of ELLs. Perhaps this is the reason that many states have a wide range of identification methods and do not rely only on one particular instrument or assessment. A look at the data on ELL identification reveals that Florida and Texas are on the lower end of the spectrum, with four methods, whereas states such as Louisiana and North Carolina employ 12 methods of ELL identification.

The Demographics of English Language Learners

In the primary and secondary education in the United States, the number of ELLs is more than 5 million, which means that ELLs represent over 10% of the entire public school population in the United States. The number itself is very substantial, but more impressive yet is the staggering rate of growth experienced in the past decade: 2.59% growth for the total K–12 population and 60.7% for the ELL students (National Clearinghouse for English Language Acquisition [NCELA], 2007). Going back more than a decade, we see that the reported number of ELLs grew by more than 160% from 1979 to 2003 (Francis et al., 2006). By looking at this remarkable rate of growth, we can see that the ascending trend regarding the ELL population will probably continue in the near future.

Today, ELLs are concentrated in six states: California, Texas, Florida, New York, Illinois, and Arizona. These six states represent over 70% of the total number of ELLs enrolled in K–12 schools in all the states and the District of Columbia. Table 3 shows the six states with the highest ELL populations enrolled in their public schools in the 2007–2008 academic year.

Table 3.   The Six States With the Highest ELL Populations, 2007–2008

State	ELL Population
California	1,553,091
Texas	701,799
Florida	268,207
New York	208,848
Illinois	175,454
Arizona	166,572

However, these statistics do not always give us the complete picture of ELL enrollment at the state level. Let us consider the ELLs enrolled in public schools in Florida. In that, state, ELLs are called LEPs and are categorized as follows:

LY = LEP students enrolled in classes specifically designed for LEP students

LN = LEP students not enrolled in classes specifically designed for LEP students

LP = Grade 4–12 LEP students for whom the reading and writing test is pending

LF = Former LEP students who exited the program in the last 2 years

LZ = Former LEP students who exited the program more than 2 years ago

In the reported statistics, LZs are considered non-LEPs, thus making the number of ELLs seem much smaller. For example, if we compare the data for the 2004–2005 and the 2005–2006 academic years with and without the LZ category, there are several serious discrepancies in the numbers.

For 2004–2005, Florida reported 299,346 ELLs, which represented 12.6% of the entire K–12 student population. If we add the LZs to this number, we have a total of 475,096 ELLs, which puts the percentage of ELLs at 20%.

For 2005–2006, the Florida Department of Education (www.fldoe.org) reported that it had 310,996 ELLs without the LZs. If we add the LZs, the actual number of ELLs is 495,092. Without the LZs in the category of ELLs, the percentage of ELLs in Florida's public school system is 13.1%; however, if the LZs are added, the percentage rises significantly, to 20.8%.

Perhaps this discrepancy makes a good argument for a specific definition of what it means to be an ELL, not just in terms of background but also in term of language proficiency. Indeed, these LZ students were exited from ESOL programs and, after monitoring, were not required to return to ESOL programs, but were they really ready to fully function at the same level as native speakers of English? Are we confident that the exit tests for ELLs are valid and reliable enough so that when ELLs pass them, they are able to fully function not only at the social language level but also at the academic language level of the content area classroom?

When we look at enrollment per educational cycles (Capps et al., 2006), elementary education enrollment nationwide is very similar to the overall ELL enrollment data. The states that have the most ELLs also have the most

ELLs enrolled in K-5. Let us take New York City as an example to see how ELL numbers are distributed based on instructional cycles. According to statistical data available at www.brooklyn.liu.edu/education/betac/resources/ELL.pdf, more than half of the total ELL population was enrolled in K-5 in the 2007–2008 school year, as seen in Table 4.

However, when elementary and secondary education population data are analyzed not in terms of percentage but in terms of growth, the states with the fastest increase in ELLs are not found among the six most populous ELL states. In the last decade, South Carolina and Kentucky experienced a growth of more than 400% in their ELL populations, and other states, like North Carolina and Tennessee, recorded a growth of more than 300%. Table 5 shows the five states with the highest increase in their ELL elementary and secondary school populations between 1995 and 2005, based on the data available at www.ets.org/Media/Conferences_and_Events/pdf/ELLsympsium/ELL_factsheet.pdf.

The population of ELLs is growing at a very fast pace all over the United States, especially at the elementary and secondary levels. It is growing not only in urban areas, but also in the rural and suburban United States. However, it is important to note that a large number of ELLs are still distributed in a few

Table 4.   ELL enrollment in New York City, 2007–2008

Instructional Cycle	Percentage ELL Population
K-5	55%
6-8	17%
9-12	28%

Table 5.   The Top Five States in ELL Growth, 1995–2005

State	K–12 ELL Growth
South Carolina	714%
Kentucky	417%
Indiana	407%
North Carolina	371%
Tennessee	369%

**Table 6.   The Top Ten Districts in ELL Enrollment,
2004–2005**

State	District	Number of ELLs	Percentage of ELLs in the District
California	Los Angeles	328,684	44%
New York	New York City	122,840	12%
Illinois	Chicago	82,540	19%
Florida	Miami-Dade	62,767	17%
Texas	Houston	61,319	29%
Nevada	Clark County	53,517	20%
Texas	Dallas	51,328	32%
California	San Diego	38,629	28%
California	Santa Ana	36,807	62%
Florida	Broward County	29,909	11%

urban school districts in a few states. Table 6 presents the ELL enrollment in the 10 largest school districts as identified by the National Center for Educational Statistics (NCES). These 10 districts enrolled 17% of all ELL students in 2005 (NCELA, 2007).

English Language Learners:
A Diverse or a Uniform Population?

The demographical statistics are very relevant for understanding growth trends, but they do not provide enough specific information to answer a very basic question: who ELL students are. To answer it, we will construct a more comprehensive representation of the background of K–12 ELLs that goes beyond numbers and percentages. We will examine where these students were born, what languages they speak, what cultures they come from, and what their socioeconomic status is.

Country of Birth

One of the many misconceptions teachers have is that all ELL students are born abroad and that most of them are recent arrivals in the United States. The statistical data of the 2000 U.S. census, available at www.census.gov, show clearly that most ELLs are born in the United States. At the elementary school level, only 24% of ELLs were first-generation immigrants, whereas 58% and 18% of ELLs were second- and third-generation immigrants. At the secondary school level, there were more ELLs who were foreign-born (44%), but the rest of the ELLs (56% of the ELL population in Grades 6–12) were born in the United States (27% for second-generation ELLs and 29% for third-generation ELLs).

If we look at Florida, which is one of the states with the highest ELL population, the statistics are in agreement with the national ones. The United States is the first country listed as country of birth by ELLs, with 53% of ELLs being born here. The second country is Cuba, with 7%, and the third one is Haiti, with 6%. In fourth place is Puerto Rico, with 5.5%, and in fifth place is Mexico, with 5.3% (www.fldoe.org).

Linguistic and Cultural Background

As for the language background of ELLs, there is a noticeable dominance of Spanish over other languages. In 2000, 76% of all ELLs enrolled at the elementary level (K–5) spoke Spanish, and 72% of all secondary education ELLs were native Spanish speakers (Capps et al., 2006). No other language represented more than 3% of all ELLs enrolled in K–12 classes in the United States. At the elementary level, the five most spoken languages after Spanish were Chinese (2.6%), Vietnamese (2.5%), Korean (1.4%), Hmong or Miao (1.3%), and French (1.1%).

At the secondary level, the order was slightly different. After Spanish, French was the most common language spoken by ELLs (3%), followed by Vietnamese (3%), Chinese (2.7%), Korean (1.6%), and Haitian Creole (1.4%).

This information could have a tremendous impact on the services provided to ELLs and on the measurement of their academic performance, especially in large-scale assessments. Although it is almost impossible to have the standardized assessments translated into all the languages that ELLs speak, if such tests were translated into Spanish (when the students' educational and language background requires it), we would be addressing the language needs of more than 70% of the entire ELL population. The question is whether such translation is an effective accommodation. We will explore this issue in Chapter 3.

In addition, school materials and parent-teacher communications translated into Spanish might be more effective in reaching out to the parents of ELLs and involving them in their children's education. Again, we are not proposing that the other languages be overlooked. Rather, if resources are limited and choices have to be made, helping more than 70% of ELL students and parents by focusing on Spanish makes a lot of economic sense (even though it is unfortunately at the expense of the other languages).

Not too long ago, one of my graduate students, who was taking an "ESOL in the Content Area" methods class, confessed at the end of the course that before taking my class, he thought all Hispanic students were alike. His rationale was that they must share a single culture since they all spoke Spanish, and he was amazed by the cultural diversity that he discovered within the Hispanic community by the time my class was over. Such an idea is very common among educators who have limited exposure to cultural diversity. It is helpful to look at the countries from which children's immigrant parents or grandparents have come in order to realize the amazing cultural diversity that one can find within a single category, such as Hispanic.

In 2000, at the elementary school level, the U.S. census (data available at www.census.gov) looked at where ELLs' mothers were born. The rationale for this choice was based on the observation that, in many instances, ELLs speak the language of their mothers. The data showed that most of the ELLs' mothers came from Mexico, followed by El Salvador, the Dominican Republic, Guatemala, and Cuba. At the secondary school level, the list of countries was Mexico, El Salvador, the Dominican Republic, Cuba, and Colombia.

It is true that in all these countries the people speak Spanish, but they do not use a generic, universally adopted version of the language. Instead, they speak versions of Spanish that display important and very visible differences, especially at the vocabulary level. For instance, in Spain, the word for "bus" is *autobus*, but in Mexico it is *camión*, and in Puerto Rico and the Dominican Republic it is *guagua*. In Chile, *guagua* means "child," so a Spanish speaker from Chile might have a potential communication problem when using this word with a Dominican or Puerto Rican Spanish speaker. Imagine the problems when tests and assessments are to be translated in Spanish!

Thus, all Hispanics speak Spanish, but they do not speak an all-encompassing, generic version of Spanish. Rather, they speak a version of the language that is in tune with the speakers' geographical, political, historical, and social context. If a native language is used in an assessment, such lexical differences between various versions of the language must therefore be taken into account by test designers, in the case of a large-scale assessment, or by classroom teachers, in the case of a classroom-based assessment.

Language is not the only criterion by which to categorize ELLs. For Black non-Hispanic ELLs, color is the separating factor, whereas Asian non-Hispanic ELLs are in the ELL category because of geographic location. Cultural diversity among ELLs within these two categories (color and geographic location) is even more evident than the case of Hispanic ELLs. The data for the mothers of Black non-Hispanics in K–12 list Jamaica, Haiti, Nigeria, Trinidad and Tobago, and Guyana as their countries of origin, whereas the data for the mothers of Asian non-Hispanic ELLs show them coming from the Philippines, Vietnam, India, China, Laos, and Korea.

The simple enumeration of the countries found in each category should make educators reconsider stereotypes attached to all ELLs found in one category. For example, based on an analysis of stereotypes linked to Asian students and available at www.ericdigests.org/2002-4/asian.html, these students are seen as great in math and science, and not interested in fun. Perhaps some of them are, but not all of them display these characteristics, given the vast within-group diversity. This should also make test designers think twice before they write a test that targets a specific group of ELLs. Test writing could be effective for ELL subgroups, but when entire groups (e.g., Hispanics or Asians) are involved, cultural and linguistic differences might be insurmountable and can negatively affect the validity and reliability of the assessment instruments.

Socioeconomic Status

The last element that will help with the construction of a comprehensive image of ELLs' backgrounds is socioeconomic status. At both the elementary and secondary level, Hispanic ELLs are more likely than other groups to come from low-income families. At the elementary level, almost 70% of ELL students with parents born in Mexico, El Salvador, the Dominican Republic, and Guatemala come from low-income families. The exception in the top five countries with the most ELL representation was Cuba, with 31% of students from low-income families.

At the secondary level, the situation is slightly better: More than 55% of ELLs with parents born in Mexico, El Salvador, and the Dominican Republic were low-income, whereas ELLs of Cuban and Colombian origin were 37% and 34% low-income, respectively. The percentages at the secondary level do look more encouraging, but it is important to note that Mexican-origin ELLs represent more than 52% of the K–12 students who have parents of Hispanic origin (60% at the elementary level and 45% at the secondary level). Therefore, it is very safe, yet unfortunate, to say that ELLs of Hispanic origin, especially ELLs of Mexican descent, do not score high on income level compared to other categories of children of immigrants.

For the Asian non-Hispanic category, the country with the most representation at both the elementary and secondary level is the Philippines, with 17% and 16% of students at the poverty level for K–5 and Grades 6–12, respectively. Table 7 shows the striking differences in income-level among major groups of immigrant-origin K–12 children.

Table 7.   Income-Level Differences of ELLs by Ethnicity

Category	K–5 Low Income	6–12 Low Income
White non-Hispanic	25%	24%
Black non-Hispanic	44%	43%
Asian non-Hispanic	33%	35%
Hispanic	66%	61%

Of particular interest is that in the White non-Hispanic category, almost 5% are children of Mexican descent. The numbers for Mexican White non-Hispanics are very similar to the numbers for Hispanics in term of economic status: 56 % of K–5 children of Mexican Whites and 46% of Grades 6–12 children of Mexican Whites came from low-income families.

U.S. Legislation Affecting English Language Learners

After the somewhat comprehensive examination of ELL backgrounds, the next question is whether the U.S. educational system has any responsibility vis-à-vis students who are LEP. Are the educational rights of this category of students protected by law in the United States? To answer this question, this section will first concentrate on the general laws concerning the education and access to education of ELLs. Then, because of the No Child Left Behind Act's significant impact on the education of ELLs at both the federal and the state levels, this very important piece of legislation will be examined in detail, with a special focus on its assessment component.

General Education Laws Concerning ELLs

The Bilingual Education Act

Also known as Title VII of the Elementary and Secondary Education Act, the Bilingual Education Act, passed by the U.S. Congress in 1968, was the first instance in which the needs of students with limited English-speaking ability were recognized at the federal level. It targeted the speaking ability of children whose dominant language was not English and whose families were low-income. The reauthorization of the act in 1974 and 1978 brought forth two important changes: The income requirements were eliminated and LEP children were specifically included in the population to be served.

The reauthorization of 1984 provided funds not only for the LEP children but also for the families of the children who were being served in family English literacy programs. In addition, it funded the development of two-way bilingual programs. The final reauthorization of the act occurred in 1994 and strongly promoted the goal of encouraging dual-language proficiency for ELLs, not just their transition to full English proficiency.

Since it was first passed in 1968, Title VII has funded basic services for ELLs, pre-service and in-service professional development programs for teachers, and grants to districts that serve ELLs.

Lau v. Nichols

Lau v. Nichols, a case brought before the Supreme Court in 1974, examined the dilemma of whether equal is fair when ELLs are involved. The plaintiffs, representing 1,800 ELLs of Chinese descent, sued the San Francisco school district for not providing English language instruction. The Supreme Court ruled in favor of the plaintiffs and stated that the San Francisco school district did not comply with Title VI of the Civil Rights Act.

According to the Supreme Court, the school district denied students of Chinese origin who did not speak English a meaningful opportunity to participate in the public school system. Providing students with equal access to desks, books, teachers, and curriculum does not translate into equal educational opportunity if the students do not speak English. When English is the mainstream language of instruction, measures must be taken to guarantee that instruction is adapted to address the linguistic and cultural characteristics of students who do not speak English.

The decision of the Supreme Court in *Lau v. Nichols* had significant and instant effects in the educational arena in the United States. It directly led to the establishment of standards for identifying ELLs, for assessing their language proficiency, and for meeting their instructional needs. In addition, even though the decision did not require any specific solution to address the limited English proficiency of ELLs, it favored the establishment of bilingual programs in states like Texas or California as a way of avoiding violations of Title VI of the Civil Rights Act.

Plyer v. Doe

Plyer v. Doe, a case presented before the U.S. Supreme Court in 1982, examined a Texas statute that denied access to education to children of illegal immigrants. The Texas statute was a 1975 revision of education laws that authorized school districts to deny enrollment to students who had not been legally admitted to the United States. The Supreme Court struck down the statute and ensured that all school-age children, whether legal or illegal immigrants, who live in the United States have the right to attend public schools. Therefore, public schools in the United States are not allowed to deny admission to students based on immigration status, to require students or parents to produce evidence of their immigration status, or to require students to provide social security numbers.

The No Child Left Behind Act: The Education and Assessment of English Language Learners

At the beginning of 2002, President George W. Bush signed the reauthorization of the Elementary and Secondary Education Act: the No Child Left Behind Act (NCLB). Congress passed it in 2001. The act, as it was at the beginning of 2010, required that all children, including ELLs, reach grade-level proficiency in English language arts and mathematics by 2014. Schools and districts risked serious consequences if ELL students, among other subgroups, did not make continuous progress toward this goal or did not show adequate yearly progress (AYP)—a standard defined by the category of students—as measured by performance on annual state tests. Titles I and III contained most of the important provisions that affect the education and assessment of ELLs.

Title I: Improving the Academic Achievement of the Disadvantaged

The purpose of Title I was "to ensure that all children have a fair, equal, and significant opportunity to obtain a high-quality education and reach, at a minimum, proficiency on challenging state academic achievement standards and state academic assessments." This purpose was to be achieved by the following:

1. Aligning curriculum, teaching, and assessment to state standards

2. Meeting the educational needs of low-achieving children from the following categories: low-income, ELLs, migratory, special education, and Indian [Native American]

3. Striving to close the achievement gap between minority and non-minority children, with a focus on low-income students

4. Holding schools accountable for not improving the academic achievement of their students

5. Focusing on improving teaching, learning, and assessment by using statewide assessment instruments aligned to state achievement and content standards

6. Promoting effective scientifically based instructional strategies and challenging academic content

7. Providing ample opportunities to teachers and administrators for professional development

8. Encouraging parental participation in the education of their children

Beginning in the third grade, Title I required schools to improve the performance of their ELLs in reading and math, as measured by state assessments. If schools constantly failed to improve the performance of their students, these schools were subject to various types of interventions, such as allowing parents to send their children to other schools or offering additional services like after-school programs. If these schools continued to show no AYP, they were to be restructured and even closed.

Title III: Language Instruction for Limited English Proficient and Immigrant Students

Title III had three parts: Part A, the English Language Acquisition, Language Enhancement, and Academic Achievement Act; Part B, the Improving Language Instructional Programs for Academic Achievement Act; and Part C, General Provisions. Part C simply involved the definition of terminology used in Parts A and B, so the discussion will concentrate primarily on Parts A and Part B.

Part A, English Language Acquisition, Language Enhancement, and Academic Achievement Act, had several purposes. First, it aimed to make sure that ELLs develop high levels of academic achievement in English and content areas, as measured by state standards. It also focused on developing, establishing, implementing, and sustaining language instructional programs and programs of English language development for ELLs. One of the purposes of this act was to prepare ELLs to enter instructional settings in which English is used exclusively. In this type of circumstance, transitional language programs, whose main purpose is to mainstream ELLs into all-English classrooms, are favored at the expense of maintenance programs that purposefully maintain proficiency in both English and the native language of ELLs.

In addition, Part A held schools and educational agencies accountable for increases not only in English proficiency but also in academic content knowledge, by requiring these agencies to show yearly measurable improvements in English proficiency and AYP for ELLs.

Part B, Improving Language Instructional Programs for Academic Achievement Act, aimed to ensure that LEP children "master English and meet the same rigorous academic standards for academic achievement [that] all children are expected to meet, including meeting challenging State academic content and student academic achievement standards." This purpose was to be fulfilled by developing and promoting accountability systems for educational programs that serve ELLs, by developing language skills and multicultural understanding, and by focusing on the development of English proficiency in ELLs and, to the extent possible, the native-language proficiency of ELLs. (However, as already noted, the purpose of language-development programs is transition to full English instructional settings.)

The Effects of the No Child Left Behind Act

NCLB has had very rigorous and ambitious goals that can exercise a great deal of influence on the education of ELLs both short-term and long-term. The law, as it was at the beginning of 2010, sought to bring every child to grade-level proficiency in math and reading by 2014. The states had to create valid testing instruments to measure the progress of all students, including ELLs. The law provided the financial support for the creation of valid measures of academic competence as well as of language proficiency, which is a positive shift from a previous focus on content only. Language proficiency in English was seen as an integral part of academic success for ELLs, and it was not separated from content proficiency in the core subject.

In 2006, 27 states were invited to work on developing reading and math tests for ELLs through a program initiated by the U.S. Department of Education. The program examined four types of testing systems geared toward ELLs: tests in English with ELL accommodations, tests that use simplified English, tests in the native language of ELL students, and tests that use the English proficiency test as a reading test. Minnesota was one of the states that developed an alternate version of its math exam for ELLs, called the Mathematics Test for English Language Learners (MTELL). This new test, in use beginning in 2007, focused on the language needs of ELLs by customizing the language of math word problems that describe real-life situations. Taking this test instead of the regular math test is helping ELLs to show what they know about math without language getting in the way.

NCLB could also have an effect on the ELLs' development of language that is associated directly with the content area curriculum, with the purpose of improving ELLs' performance on yearly statewide assessments. ELLs were required to learn the same content and pass the same exams as non-ELL students, so classroom instruction for ELLs has become more focused on both English language proficiency improvement and content area knowledge learning. In the past, language programs for ELLs concentrated mainly on language proficiency, whereas content area instruction gave more attention to core-subject academic goals. However, because of NCLB, language program teachers (English immersion or bilingual) have begun to incorporate academic content as much as possible and content area teachers have started to actively promote language proficiency development in their classrooms.

In spite of several positive effects of NCLB, the law could also create additional challenges for schools with large numbers of ELLs. Because ELLs tend to also be low-income students, these schools could be more likely to be the target of the interventions that are required by the act when performance standards are not met. In addition, because of the constant pressure to achieve the performance targets in reading and math, the quality of education might suffer. Subject areas that are ignored by state assessment might be overlooked by school administrators, who might be inclined to modify the curriculum by placing a stronger emphasis on what is tested in large-scale assessments.

We already mentioned that the law placed English proficiency, as well as the ability to fully function in an all-English environment, among its top priorities. As a result, dual-language programs that foster proficiency in both languages might be replaced by English immersion or transitional programs that have the building of English proficiency as their only purpose. Limited language proficiency in English may cause ELLs to score poorly on tests and consequently drop out because of their low grades. For example, if we look at the data on high school completion, the overall dropout rate for Hispanics is 28%. However, a closer look at the subgroups provides a better picture of Hispanic student graduation rates: Only 15% of the Hispanics who were born here drop out of high school, compared to a 44% dropout rate for foreign-born Hispanics (Thernstrom & Thernstrom, 2004). A reexamination of English language program policies and the philosophical orientation that over-emphasizes English language proficiency might prove beneficial in reducing these incredibly low graduation numbers for Hispanics.

After the passing of NCLB, there has been an increased pressure on educators to provide quality instruction to ELLs and to measure their progress according to federal standards and guidelines.

According to the 2010 version of NCLB, all children were expected to perform at grade level by 2014. Consequently, teachers, and especially content area teachers, needed to be prepared to address the language and cultural needs of their ELLs not only when they taught ELLs but also when they designed and implemented assessment techniques and instruments.

It is important to remark that NCLB will definitely undergo significant changes in the future. Some states have considered the law too rigid in its AYP approach that defines student success only through test scores. West Virginia has created an alternative measurement of school performance after its second-best school in the state failed to make AYP as defined by NCLB. Taking into account these concerns, the Obama administration has prepared a set of changes that, if approved by Congress, will change or eliminate several fundamental requirements of the law. These changes, available at the Department of Education's website (www.ed.gov), include more flexibility and an increased emphasis on student success.

The more drastic amendments center on two fundamental pillars of the NCLB law: the 2014 deadline and AYP. The Obama administration seeks the elimination of the law's 2014 deadline for bringing every student to academic proficiency. Additionally, the way schools are judged to be succeeding or failing has been under scrutiny. As a result, the Department of Education also wants to eliminate the school ratings system built on making adequate yearly progress, and implement a new system that looks to incorporate more than student test scores.

The current NCLB system in place in the spring of 2010 gives pass-fail report cards for every school each year. It does not differentiate among schools that are in chronic failure, for example, and schools that are helping low-scoring students improve. The new accountability system would divide schools into more categories, offering recognition to those that are succeeding and providing large amounts of money to help improve or close failing schools. Additionally, a new goal, replacing the 2014 proficiency deadline, would be for all students to leave high school "college or career ready." Currently more than 40 states are working on a set of new standards defining what it means to be ready for college or a career. However, these changes would have to be approved by Congress, which for years has not been able to reach an agreement on how the law should be changed.

Things to Consider

- Approximately 5 million or 10% of the U.S. student population are ELLs. Projections are showing that by 2015, ELL enrollment will double again to 10 million.

- While English learners can be found throughout the United States, they are heavily concentrated in six states: Arizona, California, Texas, New York, Florida, and Illinois.

- Despite the high concentration in six states, other states have experienced a 300% growth of ELLs in a ten-year period from 1995 to 2005. These states include Alabama, Arkansas, Indiana, Kentucky, Nebraska, North Carolina, and South Carolina.

- More than 75% of ELLs in the United States are from Spanish-language backgrounds.

- 2/3 of ELLs are U.S.-born.

- There is enormous diversity within the population of ELLs, in terms of their native-language and English language abilities, cultural background, school experiences, and socioeconomic status.

Chapter 2

Assessment: Definition, Types, and General Principles

This chapter will discuss the basic principles of assessment, with examples from the content areas to provide teachers with the knowledge that will enable them to design valid and reliable classroom-based or large-scale tests and critically examine existing and future state assessments.

What Is Assessment?

Because of the ever increasing importance placed on various statewide tests that are given to K–12 ELLs every year, many teachers tend to equate assessment with the tests they administer, whether on a large scale or in their classrooms. Test results, especially those collected through standardized instruments, certainly have critical educational consequences for students, parents, teachers, and school administrators. More and more, the scores from large-scale tests determine whether students will graduate, how much of a bonus teachers will receive, and whether schools are passing or failing in terms of performance grades.

Assessment, however, is much more than tests and test scores. Bachman (1990) identified three fundamental concepts associated with the process of assessment of student performance in the social sciences: measurement, test, and evaluation.

Measurement, which Bachman (1990) considers to be synonymous with assessment, is defined as "the process of quantifying the characteristics of persons according to explicit procedures and rules" (p. 18). This definition has three clear attributes: quantification, characteristics, and procedures and rules. Quantification deals with the process of assigning numbers to performance results. Characteristics can be either physical or mental; in assessment, researchers and practitioners are interested in mental characteristics, such as aptitude, intelligence, motivation, language proficiency, and academic knowledge. Procedures and rules are the process through which the quantification of student characteristics is conducted.

For ELLs, the clear understanding and application of such rules is critical. For example, in large-scale content area tests, most states do not have a separate testing instrument for ELLs, so they use the tests they administer to native English speakers, with specially designed ELL accommodations added. However, these accommodations are not given automatically to ELLs; they must be requested by the parents, the teachers, or the students. Yet if, for instance, the parents are not aware of the procedures and rules, they will not request the accommodation for their children, thus jeopardizing not only the validity of the assessment but also the future academic career of their children, because many of these tests are used for important educational decisions such as graduation, academic placement, and scholarships. If the teachers do not have a clear understanding of the procedures and rules, they might deny ELLs access to accommodations simply because they believe that a particular accommodation, such as reading the test questions aloud in English, is not allowed.

The second concept Bachman (1990) discusses is *test*, which he defines as "a measurement instrument designed to elicit a specific sample of an individual behavior" (p. 20). For example, content area tests are designed to measure the academic standards to which students have been exposed in the classroom and determine whether the content associated with these standards has been acquired. The test will not measure all the standards associated with a particular grade level, but it will select a representative sample of those standards for assessment. Based on this measurement and, just as important, on the quality of this measurement, educators can make inferences regarding the mastery of all the standards.

Evaluation, Bachman's (1990) third concept, is the collection of "reliable and relevant information" (p. 22). The information that is collected does not have to be exclusively quantitative. Other sources of information, such as teacher-generated narratives and checklists, can help to provide a more comprehensive picture of students and their abilities. Evaluation does not have to rely exclusively on test scores, and test scores are not always evaluative. Tests should be used to motivate students to study more or to help identify gaps in their knowledge base. However, test results should be used more as a basis for educational decisions and less as a source of information.

Assessment and English Language Learners

Assessment is a combination of all formal and informal judgments and findings that occur inside and outside a classroom. Assessment consists of a multitude of points of testing and other forms of measurement. The sum of all these points creates a holistic picture of ELLs' abilities and progress in learning English and, equally important, their mastery of content area knowledge. In other words, assessment represents a wide range of procedures that are used to gather information about what students know and, more important, are able to demonstrate (Herrera et al., 2007). It is unfortunate that standardized test scores, which are just a single measurement of ELLs' content area knowledge, are increasingly being used as the only measure of academic progress and language development for nonnative English speakers in U.S. public schools.

Moreover, until No Child Left Behind (NCLB), standardized tests did not purposefully take into account the differences that must be considered when assessing ELLs. ELLs were more of an afterthought, and it was believed that test accommodations would make the test results valid and comparable to those of their native English-speaking peers. Only recently have researchers started to analyze test accommodations for ELLs in an effort to find out whether they are valid and really contribute to the reduction of the performance gap between ELLs and native English speakers.

Fairness is one reason that educators should consider different assessment procedures and accommodations for ELLs. Nutta and Pappamihiel (2001) stated that *equal* (i.e., the same) education for ELLs does not always translate into *fair* education. Simply providing ELLs with the same test and testing conditions that are given to their native English-speaking peers does not ensure test fairness and thus equal and valid chances to measure ELLs' abilities in content areas.

This idea that equal is not always fair was recognized in *Lau v. Nicols*, the case brought before the Supreme Court in 1974 discussed in Chapter 1. The Supreme Court decided that providing the same education for ELLs without considering their cultural and linguistic differences did not give the students a fair education. Because the plaintiffs, ELLs of Chinese origin, did not have full competence in English, they were excluded from educational opportunities even though they had access to the same instruction and the same educational materials as their native English-speaking peers. Therefore, for ELLs, it is not equality to have the same instructional methods and testing instruments as the English-speaking students have, unless there are modifications and accommodations. More important, Cummins (1994) showed that ELLs still need academic and language accommodations even after they have passed language proficiency tests and are mainstreamed.

The assessment of ELLs in content areas should be different from the assessment of native English speakers in content areas. Nieto (2004) has suggested three educational implications of the *Lau v. Nichols* decision. First, educators must recognize the differences that ELLs bring to the school's educational and cultural context. In many cases, ELLs speak a different language, belong to a different culture, and have different social values. If the educational system does not recognize these differences and make the necessary adjustments in terms of instruction and assessment, ELLs will feel rejected by the schools. These feelings of rejection are easily translated into the high dropout rates that we see among ELLs nationwide.

The second implication suggested by Nieto (2004) emphasizes the strong connection between ELLs' identities and the way they experience schools in the United States. After teachers acknowledge that ELLs are different from the general student population, they must go through a process of admitting the fact that identity is a contributing factor in determining whether learning is successful or not. This has a direct implication on the design of tests or any other forms of assessment for ELLs. Tests should not be designed with lower expectations for ELLs, but any form of assessment should consider the connections among culture, identity, and learning.

The third implication focuses on the proactive approach that test designers should take when they are creating tests to be administered to the entire student population, ELLs included. Test designers must make provisions for the cultural and linguistic differences that ELLs bring to the task. There are many factors that need to be considered when teachers create assessments for ELLs in order to take into account not only of the differences between ELLs and their native-English speaking peers, but also the differences within the ELL student population. First, there are language factors. Although we noted in Chapter 1 that many ELLs come from Spanish-speaking backgrounds, the number of languages spoken by ELLs in the United States is around 400. This is important to be kept in mind when teachers decide to provide native-language accommodations for instruction and testing. Additionally, ELLs have varying levels of proficiency in English, as well as in their native language. If ELLs can converse easily in English, that does not mean they have achieved full reading and writing proficiency in English. Moreover, teachers should not assume that their ELLs have full proficiency encompassing academic language in their native language. If ELLs speak Spanish or Vietnamese, that does not mean they automatically understand written directions in Spanish or Vietnamese.

Another factor that needs to be considered is the educational background of ELLs. ELLs who are foreign-born come with very different levels of schooling in their native language. For example, there are ELLs who are refugees from conflict zones, with very little or no formal schooling in any language;

other ELLs come to the United States with a lot of formal schooling and instruction in their native language. For this latter category of students, the primary challenge is to transfer existing academic knowledge into English, whereas ELLs in the former category must learn English and academic content simultaneously. ELLs who have been enrolled in schools where English was the language of instruction also come with varying degrees of years of formal schooling in English. For example, ELLs from migrant populations may have spent many years in the U.S., but they may have experienced many interruptions due to constant moving and relocation, with adverse effect on the development of their English and academic proficiency. Last, but not least, teachers should not assume that all ELLs have had similar experiences with standardized tests, especially in the case of foreign-born ELLs. Even though the multiple choice format is prevalent in the U.S., many ELLs are unfamiliar with this form of testing, which puts them at a disadvantage in testing situations. Classroom-based assessments and state standardized tests must take into account these differences if we are to have equitable, not just equal, instruction and evaluation of the academic progress of ELLs.

The Types of Assessment

There are four ways to categorize assessment instruments and procedures: intention, purpose, interpretation, and administration. In terms of intention, an assessment can be a spontaneous comment (informal) or it can be systematic (formal). In terms of purpose, an assessment can measure the product (summative) or it can focus on the process of learning (formative). In terms of interpretation, an assessment can be used to establish the relationship between students' performance and their peers' performance (norm-referenced) or between students' performance and a body of knowledge to be mastered (criterion-referenced). Finally, in terms of administration, an assessment can be delivered at the state or national level (large scale), or it can be limited to a classroom (classroom-based). Table 8 shows the categories of assessment and the pair of types associated with each.

Informal and Formal Assessments

In terms of intention, an assessment can occur spontaneously or it can be planned well in advance. When it occurs without much planning, it is an informal assessment. For example, an informal assessment takes place when a

Table 8.   The Categories and Types of Assessment

Category of Assessment	Type of Assessment
Intention	Informal Formal
Purpose	Formative Summative
Interpretation	Norm-referenced Criterion-referenced
Administration	Classroom-based Large scale

math teacher says, "Good job" to a student who provided the correct answer to a question such as "How much is 5 divided by 10?" Informal assessment includes any type of ad hoc reactive feedback to students' performance in the classroom.

Informal assessment is important, but it does not contribute directly to the final grade that students earn. It is very different from a test that the math students would take on which the same question might appear in written form and be assigned 10 points out of a possible 100. This math test is a good example of a formal assessment. Typically, the students know about a formal assessment well in advance, and they prepare by studying for it. Formal assessment is therefore different from informal assessment in a very fundamental way: It is systematic and planned, with the intention of measuring student achievement and mastery of a battery of objectives.

Formal assessment is generally accompanied by a numerical score that reflects how well the students understood the academic content that was presented in class. Formal assessment usually consists of tests, quizzes, or term papers, but for ELLs, content area teachers may also consider portfolios or journals as more comprehensive ways of formally assessing content objectives. One frequent criticism of tests is that they draw on a limited sample of content because of time-related constraints, since they are administered during a class period or, in the case of large-scale assessments, in several hours. Because of these constraints, tests cannot assess the depth of a student's knowledge and actually measure only a very broad base of understanding. In addition, tests rely heavily on multiple choice questions. Consequently, the students are rarely required to construct answers and very seldom are asked to remember important details, which has a negative influence on the quality of the assessed knowledge (Brown, 2004).

Formative and Summative Assessments

Why assess students, and when? In terms of purpose, an assessment can focus on the process of learning rather than on the final product, which is usually an end-of-the-semester exam. When the process is the main focus, it is a formative assessment. Formative assessment is conducted throughout a course and is used to evaluate students in the process of acquiring their competencies in the academic area or in language proficiency. The goal is to provide information on how well the students have mastered the content so far, thus helping the process of instruction.

Formative assessment does not necessarily carry a grade, and it can be done by the students in the form of self-evaluations or peer evaluations or by the teacher. An example of a structured formative assessment is the following standard from Florida's science standards for Grades 3–5: *The student understands that all matter has observable, measurable properties.* This standard is operationalized into five different components, one of which is that a student knows that the weight of an object always equals the sum of its parts. If a teacher wants to know now if an ELL student has mastered this component rather than waiting till the end of the semester to find out, the assessment shown in Figure 2 can be administered.

Note that the assessment takes into account the language needs of ELLs and uses visuals to make sure that the science standard component, rather than language proficiency, is being measured through this assessment.

Summative assessment's purpose, on the other hand, is to measure what the students have learned at the end of a course. The focus here is not on the process of learning but rather on its product. Summative assessment can take the form of a final exam at the end of a course, or it can be a standardized test that is administered statewide or nationwide. The students are assigned a grade, and important educational decisions are often based on the results of these product-oriented assessment procedures.

Thus, formative assessment takes place during the instructional process to assess the ongoing effectiveness of instruction. The results can and should be used by teachers to adapt classroom instruction to ensure that the content is adequately incorporated into the students' knowledge base. In contrast, summative assessment takes place at the end of an educational cycle. The results should be used by teachers, educational administrators, and other decision makers to measure the outcome of the instructional process. Both formative and summative content area assessments increase in effectiveness when they are based on content area standards. Teaching materials and teaching strategies in the content area should be based on the same standards as the testing materials and strategies, so that aligning the tests to the academic standards will be beneficial for the students by strongly linking assessment with instruction.

Figure 2.   Sample of a Formative Assessment

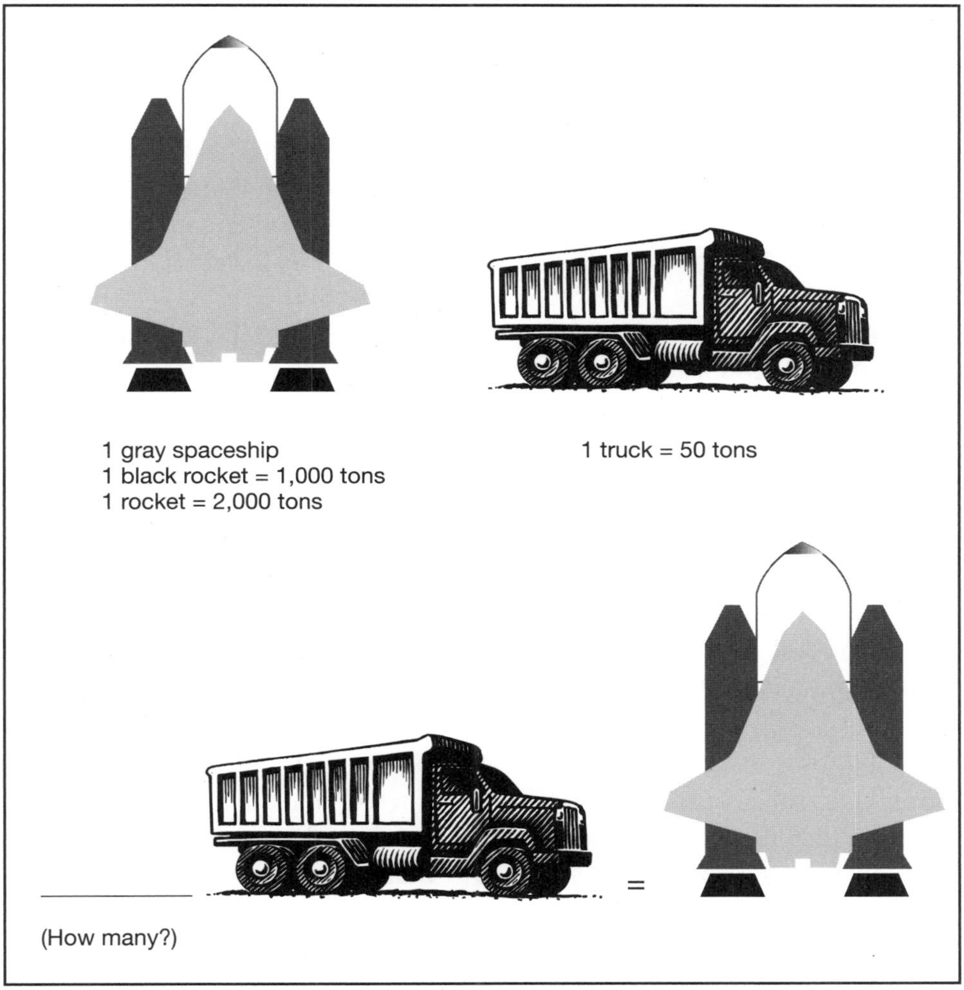

1 gray spaceship
1 black rocket = 1,000 tons
1 rocket = 2,000 tons

1 truck = 50 tons

(How many?)

Norm-Referenced and Criterion-Referenced Assessments

In terms of interpretation, in a norm-referenced assessment, each student's score is compared to the scores of a given group, or the norm. In K–12 norm-referenced assessments, the norm is usually represented by a large group of students who share similar characteristics with the students taking the assessment. Norm-referenced assessments are first administered to the norm group, and the norms, or the results of this group's performance, are used as reference points for interpreting the performance of the students who take the test in the future. The norms are the mean (the average score), the median (the middle score), the mode (the most common score), the standard deviation (how varied and spread out the group scores are), and the percentile rank (an indication of how well a particular test taker has performed compared to other group members; for example, a 78 percentile means that the test taker's score was higher than 78% of the students taking the test, but lower than 22% of the students taking the test, that day).

In a well-designed norm-referenced assessment, the scores should be distributed in a bell-shaped curve. In such a normal distribution, 50% of the scores are below the mean and 50 percent of the scores are above the mean (M). As shown in Figure 3, the scores are symmetrically distributed below and above the mean as far as two standard deviations (SD).

The scores that are obtained through norm-referenced assessments allow educators and school administrators to make only general, comparative decisions. These assessments measure a student's performance in comparison with his or her peers and show only how one student compares with other students. As a consequence, norm-referenced scores do not reveal any information about the mastery of specific academic content, so no instructional adjustment can be conducted to address the gaps in students' knowledge. Moreover, because these assessments are designed to spread the scores out in a bell-curved distribution, the test makers simply discard test items that all or a majority of the students know and keep those that can be answered correctly by approximately half of the students.

For ELLs, this can have serious consequences, because the core knowledge of a topic is likely to be purposefully ignored by the test designers. For example, in social studies norm-referenced tests, items that probe the major facts and historical events are unlikely to be selected because these items can probably be answered correctly by a large majority of the test-taking popula-

Figure 3.   An Example of a Normal Distribution

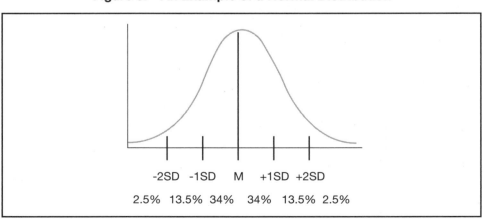

-2SD -1SD   M   +1SD +2SD

2.5% 13.5% 34%   34% 13.5% 2.5%

tion. However, with ELLs, teachers need to know if the basic knowledge has been mastered before they move to the next level of academic content.

Norm-referenced assessments are based on the assumption that the student who is taking the test has had similar educational and life experiences as the students who make up the norming sample. If this assumption is not correct, the measurement of a student's academic achievement will suffer a significant loss in validity, because it will be inaccurate and biased (Figueroa & Hernandez, 2000). ELLs are, in many cases, atypical compared to the sample population of many norm-referenced instruments.

Therefore, the equality point of view, which states that all students should be assessed using the same procedure, instrument, scoring, and interpretation, should not be applied here, because bias is generated by the fact that the student who is being assessed does not share the characteristics of the norm group. We have already discussed that equal is not always fair in the instruction of ELLs. Therefore, in order to minimize bias and to obtain valid assessments of ELLs' mastery of the academic curriculum, an equity point of view should be employed in the design and administration of norm-referenced assessments.

According to the equity view, assessment should consider a student's prior knowledge, cultural and life experiences, English and native-language proficiency, and learning style. Bias is minimized, and ELLs have a better chance of a fair and valid assessment of their abilities in the content areas when these linguistic and cultural differences, which otherwise might transform into obstacles for ELLs, are taken into consideration (Lam, 1995).

Criterion-referenced assessment takes a completely different approach in terms of interpretation and design. Criterion-referenced tests and measurements are designed with a focus on the mastery of the course content. Thus, whereas norm-referenced tests evaluate students in terms of their ranking to one another, criterion-referenced tests evaluate students in terms of their mastery of course content.

A score obtained through a criterion-referenced assessment will indicate whether the students have attained a certain degree of academic content-based proficiency. This score will not indicate a student's place or rank compared to other students who took the test, but it will definitely help the educator to decide whether a student needs more work on a particular content standard or a set of academic standards. For ELLs, criterion-referenced assessments are very beneficial from a diagnostic perspective: The scores help to identify the strengths as well as limitations of ELLs in content area subjects, so teachers can adjust their future instruction to the benefit of their students.

In order to develop a criterion-referenced assessment, an essential condition is the clear specification of both content domain and ability, or what it is necessary to demonstrate in order to show mastery of a particular academic content. A very good example of this clear specification can be found in the Criterion-Referenced Competency Tests (CRCT) that are administered in Georgia. The CRCT is designed to measure how well the students have mastered the Georgia Performance Standards and the Quality Core Curriculum. According to Georgia law, as amended by the 2000 A+ Education Reform Act, all students in Grades 1–8 are required to take the CRCT in the content areas of reading, English language arts, and mathematics. Students in Grades 3–8 are also tested in science and social studies.

The CRCT content descriptors for mathematics clearly identify the content domain and also provide the test developers with a domain description. Furthermore, they list the state standards that are associated with the domain, as well as the skills and abilities that are necessary to meet the standards.

Figure 4 shows an example of the content area descriptors for Grade 2 mathematics, obtained from the Georgia's State Department of Education (http://public.doe.k12.ga.us/ci_testing.aspx?PageReq=CITestingCRCTDesc). The descriptors are followed by an example of a CRCT item, which is adapted from the 2002 CRCT released items for second-grade students.

One word of caution for test designers: Make sure that you always test content, not language proficiency. In this item, for example, the word *hike* might be unknown to ELLs and thus create unnecessary confusion during the test. ELLs, especially those at lower levels of English proficiency, have the tendency to process print in a linear fashion. If a word is unknown, it is very difficult for low-level ELLs to use contextual cues that could help them to comprehend meaning. Therefore, since this is not a reading proficiency test, but a mathematics one, it makes more sense to substitute the word *hike* with the more commonly used *walk*.

Classroom-Based and Large-Scale Assessments

In terms of administration, assessment can take place in the classroom or can be administered in the form of state or national examinations. Classroom-based assessment is created and given primarily by teachers; it is formative and occurs on a regular basis. It is designed and scored by teachers who shape the assessment to the context of their classroom in order to gather information on the effectiveness of their instruction. Classroom-based assessment can be formal or informal, and it employs a variety of formats for student response. Its instruments include, but are not limited to, tests that are administered at the end of a unit, student portfolios, teacher checklists and narratives, class projects, and student (self- and peer) evaluations.

Let us suppose that a social studies teacher wants to assess the extent to which instruction in his or her 10th grade classroom has been effective. As

Figure 4.   CRCT Descriptors and Sample Item

Domain: Measurement

Domain Description

Measurement domain refers to students' skill in understanding length, time, and temperature and choosing an appropriate tool to measure them.

Standards Associated With Domain

M2M1: Students will know the standard units of inch, foot, yard, and metric units of centimeter and meter and will measure length to the nearest inch or centimeter.
a. Compare the relationship of one unit to another by measuring objects twice using different units each time
b. Estimate lengths and then measure to determine if estimations were reasonable
c. Determine an appropriate tool and unit for measuring

M2M2: Students will tell time to the nearest 5 minutes and know relationships of time, such as the number of minutes in an hour and hours in a day.

M2M3: Students will estimate, then measure, temperature (Fahrenheit) and determine if estimations were reasonable.

Associated Concepts, Skills, and Abilities

- Measure length to the nearest inch or centimeter
- Compare the relationship of one unit to another by measuring objects twice, using different units each time (inch, foot, yard, centimeter, and meter)
- Estimate lengths and measure to determine if estimations were reasonable
- Determine an appropriate tool and unit for measuring
- Tell time to the nearest 5 minutes and know the relationships of time, such as the number of minutes in an hour and the number of hours in a day
- Estimate, then measure, temperature (Fahrenheit) and determine if estimations were reasonable

Next Hike Starts At:

The next hike starts at 4:30. It lasts 1 hour and 20 minutes. When will the hike end?

A. 4:50

B. 5:30

C. 5:50

D. 6:10

previously noted in the discussion of formative and summative assessments, effective teaching and valid measurements of instruction should always be based on academic standards. In the state of California, several content area standards are grouped in themes for History–Social Science, and there is also a list of standards for history and social science analysis skills. Let us take the first theme, the development of modern political thought, and the first standard under this theme: *Students relate the moral and ethical principles in ancient Greek and Roman philosophy, in Judaism, and in Christianity to the development of Western political thought.* This standard, coded as WH10.1, is further divided into three more specific standards:

- WH10.1.1. Analyze the differences in Judeo-Christian and Greco-Roman views of law, reason and faith, and the duties of the individual.

- WH10.1.2. Trace the development of the Western political ideas to the rule of law and illegitimacy of tyranny, using selections from Plato's *Republic* and Aristotle's *Politics.*

- WH10.1.3. Consider the influence of the U.S. Constitution on political systems in the contemporary world.

A classroom-based assessment can take many forms. For example, after a presentation on Greek and Roman societies in class, the teacher may ask students to work in groups to create a Venn diagram through which they compare and contrast Greek and Roman societies (WH10.1.1). A Venn diagram contains two overlapping circles that correspond to the two elements that are to be analyzed by the students, in this case Greek and Roman societies. The characteristics that belong to only one category are listed in the corresponding circle, whereas the features that the two have in common are listed in the overlapping section, shown in Figure 5. The assessment of this activity can be done in the form of a rubric, also shown in the figure.

The teacher can use all the Venn diagrams that have been generated by the students to create a list of similarities and differences of the two societies examined. After the list is discussed in class with the students, the teacher can move to the next level and ask the students to brainstorm how these two societies have influenced Western society in general and the United States in particular (WH10.1). Then, the teacher can use a similar diagram to compare and contrast Judaism with Christianity and, finally, to identify the differences between the Judeo-Christian and Greco-Roman views of law, reason and faith, and the duties of the individual, as required by WH10.1.1.

Figure 5.   A Venn Diagram and Its Rubric

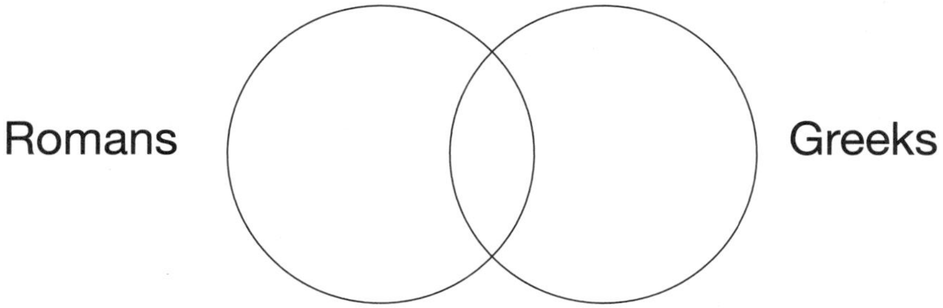

Romans   Greeks

In your group, compare Greek and Roman societies, taking into account their views on the following categories: law, faith, and the duties of the individual. List the similarities in the overlapping area. Make sure you have at least two similarities and two differences for each category.

Group members:_____

Category	Law	Faith	The individual
Number of correctly identified similarities			
Number of correctly identified differences			
Total number of points			

Comments: _____
_____
_____

Large-scale assessments are usually created by external agencies and take the form of standardized tests. These instruments are summative in nature and aim to measure students' performance at the end of an instructional cycle. Because they are administered to a large number of students, the format is limited to tests in which a large majority of the questions are multiple choice and short answer. Large-scale assessments include state and national tests, standard portfolios, tests administered at the end of the course, and district norm-referenced tests.

The same social studies standard that we used above for exemplifying a classroom-based assessment of student knowledge in social studies has also been used in creating items for the California Standards Test (CST). The CST, a standardized test, is required for the following content areas:

- English language arts, Grades 2–11

- Mathematics, Grades 2–9

- Science, Grades 5, 8, and 10 (life science)

- History–Social Science, Grades 8, 10 (world history), and 11 (U.S. history)

The released items for the CST for History–Social Science are a series of 60 multiple choice questions; however, the document (available at www.cde.ca.gov/) mentions that the released questions represent only some ways in which the standards are assessed through CST. The 10th grade standard mentioned above is tested through a series of multiple choice questions, shown in the three items in Figure 6, adapted from the released 10th grade History–Social Science test questions. All three questions pertain to standard WH10.1.2 (*Trace the development of the Western political ideas to the rule of law and illegitimacy of tyranny, using selections from Plato's* Republic *and Aristotle's* Politics).

These types of items are very difficult for ELLs who have low-proficiency levels in English. First, the sentence structure of the questions is very complex, not at all adapted to the language needs of ELLs at low levels of proficiency. Second, the vocabulary might be very difficult for ELLs. Third, the absence of any visuals clearly adds another hurdle to the ability of ELLs to comprehend and answer these types of social studies items.

The Principles of Assessment

Do tests measure content knowledge accurately? Do they cost too much? Do students need a lot of time to take them? Are the responses dependable? In the current test-driven educational context, teachers and administrators have asked themselves these questions, expressing their concerns about the effectiveness of tests, especially those that are administered on a large scale, either by individual states or nationwide. The construct of test effectiveness can be discussed by looking at its components, or principles. These principles can be applied not only to state and national tests but also to all types of assessments that have been explored in this chapter.

Figure 6. Three Test Questions for Standard WH10.1.2

- Which of the following is a concept from classical Athens that is central to Western political thought today?

a. Individual achievement, dignity, and worth are of great importance.
b. Individuals should fight against nature and society to achieve greatness.
c. Individuals play an insignificant role in shaping ideas and society.
d. Individual recognition harms societal progress.

- Who believed that an ideal society should be controlled by a class of philosopher-kings?

a. Plato
b. Thomas Aquinas
c. Lao-tzu
d. Muhammad

- "He who trusts any man with supreme power gives it to a wild beast, for such his appetite sometimes makes him: passion influence those in power, even the best of men, but law is reason without desire." —Aristotle

Which feature of modern Western democratic government reflects Aristotle's view given above?

a. The power of the courts to review the law
b. The direct election of the members of the Congress
c. The requirement that government actions must adhere to the law.
d. The granting of emergency powers to the chief executive

There are five major principles of assessment: validity, reliability, practicality, equivalency, and washback.

Validity

The American Psychological Association (1985) defines *validity* as the extent to which the inferences or educational decisions that are made based on test scores are meaningful, appropriate, and useful. Test scores themselves thus have to be meaningful. That is, they must reflect a student's individual ability in a particular area and make sure that the test does not measure anything else. Therefore, when determining how meaningful test scores are, test designers should be able to demonstrate that the results that are obtained by the students who are taking the test are not affected by factors external to the testing instrument itself. When test scores are affected by errors of measurement, they are not valid and cannot provide any solid evidence of a student's ability in a certain academic area.

For ELLs, these external sources of error are referred to by Genesse and Upshur (1996) as *input factors*. Examples of input factors that may drastically affect the validity of an assessment are prior educational background, language and academic proficiency, class size, motivation, and instructional time.

Suppose that a test does measure a specific ability for a specific academic area. The next question is whether the test (or any other type of assessment) is appropriate. Is a math test that has been designed for monolingual English speakers appropriate to use for gathering information on how well ELLs have mastered grade-level math content? Those test results are probably not going to accurately depict the ELLs' actual math competence if no accommodations were allowed and the test was administered without any modifications to ensure that input factors were minimized. Moreover, the usefulness of those test results is questionable. If educators use the results for academic placement, they might misplace a student and erroneously assume a lack of content knowledge, simply because the test did not accurately measure how much math ELLs know.

Math was selected as an example because quite a few items on math tests are word problems with very few math symbols or figures. Mathematics is often called the universal language. To grasp how universal math is on tests and to understand ELLs' frustration when taking such tests, please consider:

كم يكون اثنان و اثنان؟

The language used is Arabic; this is a very simple math problem. Instead of math symbols and numbers, words are used. If Arabic is unknown, it is very difficult to determine what is being asked. There is no math notation that might help. However, if a student who does not know Arabic sees this translation of the problem into mathematical symbols and numbers, it will be:

$2 + 2 = ?$

Even when numbers are used, language can still obstruct the validity of an assessment. This is an example in Romanian that uses numbers:

Cît fac 5 împărțit la 5?

In this case, it seems a little easier because Romanian and English share the Latin alphabet and there are numbers in the question. However, all these factors still do not help people who do not know Romanian unless they see the math translation:

$5 / 5 = ?$

There are several ways of establishing the validity of a test. The first is *content validity*, which occurs when the assessment samples the content about which conclusions are to be drawn and when it requires students to perform the behavior that is being measured (Hughes, 2003). Let us look at this test item:

Which of the following atoms has six valence electrons?

A. Magnesium (Mg)

B. Silicon (Si)

C. Sulfur (S)

D. Argon (Ar)

This chemistry test item demonstrates content validity because it is based on chemistry curricular standards and the content covered in a chemistry class in which the students were taught how to use the periodic table to determine the number of electrons available for bonding. In other words, this chemistry test item is testing chemistry content that is grade appropriate, and it will reveal how well students have mastered this specific ability in a specific content area.

Another way to establish the validity of an assessment is *construct validity*, which examines whether the underlying theories, hypotheses, or models that are intended to be tested are indeed being measured thorough the assessment instrument. Test designers and classroom teachers should consult state and national standards when creating large-scale or classroom-based assessments. For example, in biology, genetics is a construct that must be assessed. How can this construct be operationalized as test items in a large-scale assessment? Consider:

Which of the following best describes *meiosis*?

A. It is carried out in all tissues that require cell replacement.

B. It occurs only in cells in the reproductive structures of the organism.

C. It happens in all tissues except the brain and the spinal cord.

D. It is the first stage of mitosis.

This question was selected from the released items of the California Standards Test for Biology (www.cde.ca.gov/). Figure 7 shows how the item was created, and it establishes a direct link between the item and the construct to be tested, genetics.

Figure 7.   Construct Validity for a Genetics Question

Construct: Genetics

B12. Mutation and sexual reproduction lead to genetic variation in a population
(One of the four genetics standards in the California Standards for Biology)

B12.a. Students know that meiosis is an early step in sexual reproduction in which the pairs of chromosomes separate and segregate randomly during cell division to produce gametes containing one chromosome of each type.

B12.b. Students know that only certain cells in a multicellular organism undergo meiosis.

B12.c. Students know how random chromosome segregation explains the probability that a particular allele will be in a gamete.

B12.d. Students know that new combinations of alleles may be generated in a zygote through the fusion of male and female gametes (fertilization).

B12.e. Students know why approximately half of an individual's DNA sequence comes from each parent.

B12.f. Students know the role of chromosomes in determining an individual's sex.

B12.g. Students know how to predict possible combinations of alleles in a zygote from the genetic makeup of the parents.

(California Standards for Biology)

Which of the following best describes *meiosis*?

A. It is carried out in all tissues that require cell replacement.

B. It occurs only in cells in the reproductive structures of the organism.

C. It happens in all tissues except the brain and spinal cord.

D. It is the first stage of mitosis.

(Test item based on Biology Standard B12.b)

Because of the clear connection between the standards and the content of the test, this test item demonstrates construct validity. However, its validity might be compromised when ELLs are taking the test. The state of California does not have a separate content area test for ELLs, and this biology item could still be difficult to comprehend without any language modifications or support. There are no visuals to accompany the question, and ELLs are presented with a set of prewritten answers, which can easily be misinterpreted if the vocabulary is not familiar. A more valid—but, unfortunately, more costly—way of assessing the concept of meiosis is an open-ended question, such as "What is meiosis?"

The third way to establish the validity of an assessment is *criterion validity*, which is a method of cross-checking the validity of an assessment instrument. For example, a test that is designed by a teacher to be used in the classroom has criterion validity if the results are similar to the results of another assessment instrument of the same criterion, or subject matter. If a student in a physics class obtains a score of 80 out of 100 on a classroom-based end-of-semester test, and this student obtains a similar score on a standardized test that is administered statewide, then this similarity in scores is evidence that the classroom-based test has criterion validity.

This type of validity can be used as a concurrent or a predictive means of verifying validity. The two assessment instruments can be administered at the same time, or an educator can predict student performance on one assessment based on the results of the other assessment. However, with ELLs, criterion validity is very difficult to demonstrate. Classroom-based instruments often incorporate effective accommodations for ELLs that alleviate the language barriers for these students and that also allow ELLs to provide answers in alternative formats. Standardized content area assessments, however, rely heavily on language ability and allow little variety in how the answer may be given, because large-scale assessments usually favor a test format in which most questions are multiple choice and short answer.

Besides these three major types of validity, there are other types of validity that are not as important. One example is *face validity*. A test or any other form of assessment has face validity if it looks as if it is going to measure the knowledge or the ability it claims to measure (Mousavi, 2002). A math test has face validity if it appears, at a glance, to be measuring students' knowledge of math concepts and not of music or history ones.

Reliability

According to the American Psychological Association (1985), *reliability* means that a test is free of errors of measurement. Validity focuses on an error-free measure of ability alone; however, student performance can be affected by many other factors, such as fatigue or anxiety. A reliable test minimizes the effect of these factors and is consistent and dependable. If a student takes the same test on two different occasions and the scores differ significantly, these scores cannot be considered reliable indicators of that student's ability. Therefore, a reliable test is a consistent measure that stays consistent regardless of the time, the test format, raters, and other characteristics of the testing environment. There are three different types of reliability: student reliability, rater reliability, and test administration reliability (Brown, 2004).

In *student reliability*, the students themselves affect the reliability of a test through such factors as illness, fatigue, personal problems, or other psychological factors. One way to ensure student reliability is to make sure that the students are in good health and do not have any reasons to be distracted from the test's tasks, thus making the scores unreliable.

In *rater reliability*, the scoring process affects the consistency of the scores. For a multiple choice test, there is only one correct answer per item, so rater reliability is not an issue. However, assessment instruments do not rely exclusively on multiple choice, true-false, or other questions for which only one correct answer is accepted. Figure 8 shows an example of a short-answer question from the Florida Comprehensive Assessment Test (FCAT) for Grade 5 science (http://fcat.fldoe.org/):

With such an item, in which the test takers do not have a list of possible answers to choose from, the reliability of the scores can be negatively affected by human error or subjectivity. *Interrater bias* occurs when two or more raters come up with significantly different scores due to their inexperience, fatigue, or lack of concentration, or simply because they did not pay attention to the scoring criteria. Moreover, the scoring criteria themselves may be insufficiently developed, or they may be too vague, thus leaving too much room for interpretation. If the two scorers do not apply the same standards when scoring an item like the one from the Science FCAT, there is strong evidence of a lack of interrater reliability.

Rater reliability issues can appear not only when two or more raters are involved in scoring but also when only one person scores the assessments. This is called *intrarater bias*, and it is most commonly found with classroom-based assessments (tests or assignments) that are graded solely by the classroom teacher. Such bias within one person occurs because of unclear or too general scoring criteria, fatigue, or lack of attention. It is also very common for classroom teachers to grade the tests of academically good students more subjectively, because they expect these students to do well on tests. There are ways to ensure intrarater reliability—that one rater would give the same score to a test in two weeks that he or she gave to it today. Perhaps the best method is to grade all the assessments in one sitting at the same time of day with-

Figure 8.   Example of a Short-Answer Science Question

After a visit to the Grand Canyon in Arizona, Jamie wondered how a river could carve such a deep canyon. Her grandfather created a model to show the formation of the Grand Canyon. He took a glass pan and filled it with tightly packed soil. He raised the pan slightly at one end. Then he took a beaker filled with water and slowly began to pour it on the raised end of the pan. He filled the beaker with water several times and repeated the process. Every time he poured more water onto the soil, the water flow would form deeper gaps along its path in the soil.

Part A. Describe the similarities between the formation of the Grand Canyon and Jamie's grandfather model.

_____

_____

_____

_____

_____

_____

Part B. The Grand Canyon was shaped by other factors not demonstrated in the model. Identify and describe two of these factors.

_____

_____

_____

_____

_____

_____

out reading the names of the students;another is to carefully design scoring rubrics that are very detailed and specific and leave no room for unnecessary interpretation and bias.

If assessment conditions do not change, and the administration of the assessment is consistent, then the assessment has *test administration reliability*. Noisy environments can provide unwanted distraction and can provoke a lack of concentration in students, thus affecting the scores. Variations in temperature, the familiarity of the environment, and other similar factors could negatively influence the reliability of the scores. It is thus important to make sure that test conditions are the same for students who take a test on Monday morning and students who take the same test on Thursday afternoon, if test administration reliability is to be demonstrated.

Practicality

Besides being valid and reliable, an assessment must also be practical. That is, its creator must take into consideration the cost and time demands that are placed on teachers, students, and administrators. Brown (2004) identifies several characteristics of *practicality.* First, a test must stay within reasonable financial parameters by not being prohibitively expensive. Second, the time and effort it takes to administer the test must be appropriate. If an assessment is difficult to administer, demands special training for the proctors, or requires expensive or not readily available supplemental equipment, then that assessment lacks practicality. Third, the scoring methods must be clear, specific, and time-efficient.

The best way to assess a certain skill is to directly test that skill. If we want to assess academic writing, the most valid method of assessment is to actually have students put together a portfolio that contains a selection of the students' most representative writing samples in the content area. However, such an assessment instrument is problematic because of cost and time. Therefore, in spite of the fact that validity is very strong in such an assessment, this has to be balanced with practicality. Such an assessment may be used at the classroom level, but for a state or a national assessment, a different instrument would have to be employed.

An example of an instrument that tests writing ability directly is the Florida Comprehensive Assessment Test (FCAT) in writing, in which students are required to produce a timed essay that is assessed on scale from 0 to 6. Starting in 2005, FCAT added a new section of multiple choice questions to test grammar, punctuation, and the ability to organize one's writing. Figure 9 shows an example of a multiple choice question from the Grade 10 writing test.

In spite of the practical aspect of this indirect way of testing writing, in April 2008 the state of Florida decided to eliminate multiple choice questions and employ only the timed essay as the means of assessing the writing ability of K-12 Florida students. If the multiple choice items had prevailed, it would have been an instance in which the desire to make the assessment more practical and inexpensive would have affected the construct validity of the test in a negative way.

Figure 9.   Grade 10 Writing Test Sample

Read the article "A Popular Dance." Choose the word or words that correctly complete Questions 1–3.

In the early part of the (1)_____ century, a popular dance called Jarabe Tapatio developed in Mexico. The dance tells a story of romance (2)_____ a man and a woman. The dancers tap and stamp their feet in a rhythmic pattern as they weave around each other, always a little distance apart. Toward the end of the dance, the male dancer throws down a large hat called a sombrero, and the female dancer dances around it. This part of the dance is called "The Dove" because the dancers' steps (3)_____ like doves chasing each other. Finally, the female dancer picks up the hat and puts it on her head, thus letting the male dancer know she likes him. The Jarabe Tapatio was proclaimed the national dance of Mexico in 1920.

1. Which answer should go in blank (1)?
   A. twenteth
   B. twentieth
   C. twentyeth

2. Which answer should go in blank (2)?
   A. among
   B. between
   C. toward

3. Which answer should go in blank (3)?
   A. look
   B. looks
   C. looked

Equivalency

An assessment has the property of *equivalency* if it is directly based on curricular standards or instructional activities. Specifically, equivalency determines in what ways assessment design is influenced by teaching. In statewide assessments, equivalency is evident when the assessment is based first and foremost on content area standards. Consider the following item from a statewide standardized test, Georgia's Criterion-Referenced Competency Test for 10th grade social studies.

Which of the following is a characteristic of the Okefenokee Swamp?

A. It is located in the Piedmont region.

B. It has the most precipitation in the state.

C. It is famous for its hydroelectric potential.

D. It is the largest freshwater marsh in the state.

When we look at Georgia's social studies standard S8G, *The student will describe Georgia with regard to physical features and location*, it is clear this item is based on it.. This standard is further described as follows:

   a. Locate Georgia in relation to region, nation, continent, and hemisphere.

   b. Describe the five geographic regions of Georgia; include the Blue Ridge Mountains, Valley and Ridge, Appalachian Plateau, Piedmont, and Coastal Plain.

   c. Locate and evaluate the importance of key physical features on the development of Georgia; include the Fall Line, Okefenokee Swamp, Appalachian Mountains, Chattahoochee and Savannah Rivers, and barrier islands.

   d. Evaluate the impact of climate on Georgia's development.

The social studies test item undoubtedly addresses (c), thus establishing an obvious standard-assessment equivalency. Furthermore, the teachers are basing their instruction on state standards, and the educational materials are based on these standards as well. Therefore, by extrapolation, this item should have instructional equivalency. However, such equivalency may be questioned if the teachers did not use the multiple choice format in their classroom-based assessment. It does not mean that their assessments were invalid; it simply means that the students may be unfamiliar with this type of format, thus making the test less reliable.

Can assessment influence instruction? If the answer is yes, in what manner?

Washback

Washback is the term that educators use to indicate the effect that an assessment has on instruction and student learning. Washback can be either positive or negative. When it is positive, it complements and strengthens teaching and learning. When it is negative, it adversely affects the quality of instruction and student learning. In large-scale assessments, washback is the effect that standardized tests have on instruction—specifically, how students prepare before taking a test.

Teaching to the test is an example of negative washback. More and more teachers are resorting to using standardized test items in their instruction, sometimes exclusively. Exposure to standardized test items is certainly not harmful for students, but it is very detrimental when the test drives the instruction instead of the other way around. The blame cannot be assigned solely to teachers, however. Teaching to the test is a reaction to the excessive importance that has been placed on standardized test scores, an emphasis that is ever increasing with NCLB.

Another negative washback of standardized tests is cramming for tests. A few weeks before a mandatory high-stakes statewide test, it is common to see students practicing standardized content area test items during art class, for instance. Math scores count for teacher bonuses, school grades, and graduation, whereas art classes do not. Again, the reason for this is the overwhelming importance that has been assigned to standardized mandatory large-scale assessments.

Assessment can and should generate positive washback, especially in classroom-based assessments. The challenge is to create assessment instruments that will positively influence instruction and student learning. Test results should be used by teachers to assess the quality of their instruction and identify gaps in students' content area knowledge. Learning can also be enhanced by providing extensive comments on test performance. If a test, a quiz, or a homework assignment is returned to the students with just a grade and no comments on student performance, such washback is clearly negative, because it does not inform the students about the strengths and weaknesses of their acquired knowledge. Rubrics can be of great help, and students can inform themselves about their academic progress by interpreting their scores based on these rubrics. It is also very helpful for classroom content area teachers to share the assessment procedures (e.g., rubrics, criteria, checklists) with the students, thus allowing them to be better prepared when taking those assessments.

In conclusion, as noted in Chapter 1, there is a documented increase in the number of ELLs in the K–12 classroom in the United States. Gottlieb (2006) states that the assessment of ELLs' language proficiency and content area knowledge should be fair, relevant, comprehensive, and inclusive. Assessment is not and should not be considered an isolated activity that is conducted only at the end of an instructional cycle and that is separated from teaching. Rather, it is part of a mechanism in which academic standards and language-proficiency standards are at the center and inform both instruction and assessment, as shown in Figure 10.

Figure 10. An Assessment Mechanism for the Language and Academic Needs of ELLs

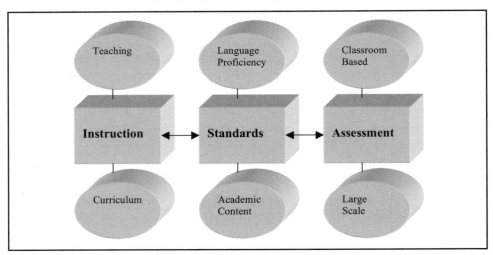

Things to Consider

- When developing or evaluating assessments, content area teachers should use the following questions based on the principles of assessment:

1. Validity: Does the assessment measure what it is suppose to measure?

2. Reliability: Does the assessment generate consistent results over time and among different groups of students?

3. Practicality: Is the administration of the assessment reasonable in terms of time and cost?

4. Equivalency: Does the assessment connect with the curriculum and class activities?

5. Washback: Does the assessment have an impact on instruction?

- When assessing ELLs, content area instructors should take into account ELLs':

1. large diversity in language background

2. wide range of proficiency in the students' native language and in English, paying close attention to their academic language proficiency in both languages

3. different degrees of formal schooling in the students' native language and in English, a range that can drastically influence the rate of academic language acquisition in English

4. experiences with standardized testing

5. acculturation to U.S. mainstream culture

Chapter 3

Large-Scale Assessment in the Content Areas and English Language Learners

This chapter will analyze large-scale assessment instruments in the content areas and how they address the needs of ELLs. The focus will be on test modifications and accommodation for ELLs as well as on research-based recommendations for test designers to help them develop assessments instruments that will measure the academic progress of ELLs in a valid and effective manner.

Legislation and Assessment: General Considerations

In the current U.S. educational setting, most districts and schools are held accountable by some sort of large-scale, usually standardized, assessment. Because more and more federal funds are distributed proportionally based on the results of such assessment programs, this trend in accountability is likely to become more prevalent in the next few years.

The No Child Left Behind Act (NCLB) has required that all students demonstrate a high level of proficiency in English language arts and mathematics by 2014. As we observed in Chapter 1, the 2014 deadline is very likely to be abandoned. However, the idea of accountability and rewarding students who make visible academic progress will still be very much at the core of any changes in legislation. It is true that tests will not be the only metric used for evaluating schools and students, but they will still be a very important component of evaluation. ELLs and all other students will be required to show that they are making progress, with or without using the AYP guidelines. Therefore, the results of statewide tests in reading and content areas will play be a significant part in determining whether or not students, ELLs included, are learning. It is important to note that the required level of proficiency in these core areas presents quite a challenge for all students in schools, but even more so for ELLs. ELLs are struggling to learn academic content *and* English, and they must show quick progress in both because the U.S. educational system allows for a catch-up period that is generally limited to two years.

It is increasingly important to consider ELLs in designing and implementing large-scale assessments. Chapter 1 showed that the number of ELLs in K–12 has grown rapidly in recent years. The growth has been not only rapid but also steady. The enrollment data of the 1994–1995 and 2004–2005 school years show that the population growth of all students in K–12 has remained steady at 2.59%. However, the population of ELLs rose by more than 60% (NCELA, 2007). Of particular interest is that in the years leading up to 2000, the ELL population grew most rapidly in the elementary grades (Kindler, 2002). However, more recent data show that ELL secondary school population growth has surpassed ELL elementary school population growth: ELL enrollment at the secondary level in the past decade increased by 64%, while enrollment at the elementary level increased by 46% (Capps et al., 2006).

Before the new federal regulations contained in No Child Left Behind (NCLB), the states were not required to include ELLs in their accountability plans. Consequently, there was very limited data available at the state level on ELLs' actual academic and linguistic progress. However, this situation has changed—first with the passage of Goals 2000 (H.R. 1804), which stipulated that standards and assessments must apply to all students, including ELLs. Furthermore, starting with the school year 2000–2001, each state was required to have a testing instrument that not only included ELLs but also made sure that these students would make adequate yearly progress (AYP) (Menken, 2000).

These accountability requirements were reinforced and extended through NCLB, passed by Congress in 2001. With this legislation, the states are now held responsible for the progress of ELLs in the content areas as well as in English language proficiency. Moreover, the states must disaggregate the data that are obtained through their large-scale assessments to show AYP for ELLs. Even if AYP is no longer the metric used for measuring progress, its replacement will not eliminate the large-scale assessments states use for measuring progress because accountability is a key word in the proposed changes to NCLB.

This increased level of accountability for the ELL population helps educators and school administrators to better understand the academic needs of ELLs. However, there have been voices in the field that have questioned the quality of the standardized assessments that are applied to ELLs —specifically, whether the results from such large-scale tests are valid and reliable (Abella, Urritia, & Shneyderman, 2005). To address validity issues, all states have generated accommodation policies for ELLs when they are taking standardized large-scale tests.

A Survey of Large-Scale Accommodations for English Language Learners

Before examining the research on ELL accommodations, it will be beneficial to define what an accommodation is and to explore the individual state policies on accommodations that target ELLs.

The Definition of Accommodation

An *accommodation* is the support that is provided to ELLs to help them access the English content of the assessment, thus enabling them to better demonstrate what they know academically.

According to Butler and Stevens (1997), the support for ELLs may be divided into two categories: modifications of the test itself or modifications of the test procedure. Modifications of the test include bilingual translations, glossaries (either in English or the student's native language), and/or simplified text. Modifications of the test procedures include flexible time limits, flexible settings, and/or the reading and explanation of the directions.

Koenig and Bachman (2004) addressed this somewhat broad categorization of accommodations by organizing them into four categories instead of two: presentation, response, time and scheduling, and setting. Presentation accommodations involve, for instance, translation of the directions and translation of the test into the student's native language. Response accommodations allow ELLs to respond in the native language or in both the native language and English. Time and scheduling accommodations give ELLs extra breaks or extended testing sessions over multiple days. Setting accommodations include small-group, separate-room, and individual administration of the test.

Nevertheless, even a four-category system is still relatively broad. It is beneficial to distinguish the types of accommodations even further in an effort to better serve ELLs by eliminating any source of ambiguity and confusion.

Thus, Pappamihiel and Mihai (2010) proposed a six-category system: time and scheduling, location, directions, presentation, support, and response. Time and scheduling accommodations include schedule changes and additional time. Location is basically equivalent to setting and includes preferential seating and a private setting. Direction accommodations include giving directions in the student's native language and reading the directions aloud. Presentation accommodations include bilingual, audio, and video version of the test. Support refers to aids like dictionaries and computers. Response accommodations include the use of the student's native language and allowing the student to point to the responses in English.

Abedi, Hofstetter, and Lord (2004) focus their attention on the effectiveness of ELL accommodations. They state that effective accommodations should level the playing field for ELLs. They suggest that test modifications should help ELLs to overcome the language barrier so that the test is a measure of their academic content knowledge and not of their language proficiency.

An example of this would be using a specialized glossary rather than a standard dictionary. For example, in English there are several definitions for *draw*. Let us suppose that a test prompt asks the students to "draw a conclusion." A regular dictionary contains at least 15 distinct definitions for this word in its transitive verb form and at least 10 definitions for this word in its intransitive verb form. A native speaker of English would probably need no help in identifying the correct meaning of the word, but an ELL could be easily confused and overwhelmed by the large number of possibilities. ELLs may interpret the meaning as "to sketch a conclusion," so they might attempt to formulate their answer as a picture rather than in words. This would affect test validity, since such an answer cannot be assessed properly by test raters. A specialized glossary would proactively ensure test validity by supplying only the definition that is appropriate to that context. Thus, the ELL is aided by that accommodation, but nothing is withheld from the native speaker. An accommodation levels the playing field for ELLS but does not give them an unfair advantage over their English-proficient peers.

ELLs' Access to Accommodations

Before discussing the accommodations that are allowed for ELLs, it is important to investigate the decision-making process that determines the access that ELLs have to these accommodations. Francis et al. (2006) identify several criteria that are used in state policies for addressing two major issues of ELL accommodations. First, the states must determine which ELLs should have the right to take state tests with accommodations. Second, the states also must establish which accommodations should be used with which groups of ELLs.

For access to ELL accommodations, research (Francis et al., 2006) on state policies reveals 10 criteria that can be arranged into the following four categories: language, academic, time, and opinion. The language criteria are (a) language proficiency in English, (b) language proficiency in the ELL's native language, (c) the language of instruction that is used in a particular educational institution, and (d) program placement. The academic criteria are (e) the academic background of ELLs in their native language(s), and (f) their performance on other tests. The time criteria are (g) the length of time that an ELL has been in the United States or in English-speaking schools, and (h) the length of time that an ELL has been in a particular state's schools. The opinion criteria are (i) a parent's or guardian's opinions about whether an ELL needs test accommodations, and (j) the teacher's observations or recommendations. Table 9 lists the 10 criteria in their categories and the number of states that are implementing them.

The 10 criteria are used to determine not only the eligibility of ELLs but also the types of accommodations that might be appropriate for these students. Many states put forth additional criteria to be considered in the selection of ELL accommodations.

The first additional criterion is that only accommodations that are used during classroom instruction are to be used during assessment. The second additional criterion is that the accommodations to be implemented should not compromise the validity of the assessment. The third additional criterion is that the accommodations should be based on the individual needs of the ELL students.

Table 9.   State Implementation of Accommodations Criteria

Category	Criterion	Number of States Implementing It
Language	English proficiency	23
	ELL native-language proficiency	7
	Primary language of instruction	2
	Language program placement	5
Academic	Academic background in native language	3
	Performance on other tests	2
Time	Time in the U.S. or English-speaking schools	5
	Time in state's schools	3
Opinion	Parent or guardian opinion or permission	3
	Teacher observation or recommendation	2

These additional criteria are quite difficult to follow, however. For example, if teachers are not involved in the decision process for selecting the appropriate test accommodations for their ELL students, it is very difficult for the test administrators to assess which accommodations have been used in the classroom and which have not. It is thus important to identify the state-level decision makers for ELL accommodations.

It is rather surprising that only 22 states specifically name the decision makers for their ELL accommodations. There are five categories of decision makers: language acquisition professionals, general education teachers, parents (or students or community members), test coordinators or administrators, and school administrators (Francis et al., 2006). Table 10 lists these five categories with their 12 different decision makers and the number of states that use them.

We have discussed who is eligible for ELL accommodations and who decides this eligibility at the state level. Next, let us look at the state tests that ELLs are required to take and the accommodations that are allowed for them.

A State-by-State Description of ELLs and Large-Scale State Assessment Accommodations

These descriptions focus on content area tests. In many instances, it is very possible that content area teachers have limited exposure to or are completely unfamiliar with the set of accommodations legally available for ELLs. We have

Table 10.   Decision Makers for Accommodations at the State Level

Category	Decision Makers	Number of States Using Them
Language acquisition professionals	ESL or bilingual teachers of student	9
	Other ESL or bilingual teachers	3
	Interpreter	1
General education teachers	ELL classroom or content area teachers	11
Parents, students, community members	ELL parents or guardians	11
	ELL students	4
	Community members	4
Test coordinators or administrators	Test administrators	5
	Reading specialists	3
	Guidance counselors	4
School administrators	Principals	9
	Other school or district officials	5

noted that accommodations are not automatically made available to ELLs. Therefore, content area teachers should be very familiar with what test modifications ELLs are allowed to use when they take state-sanctioned tests so that teachers can request these accommodations for their ELL students. Additionally, it is important to remember that ELL students need to be very familiar with an accommodation in order for it to be effective. Therefore, content area teachers must know what accommodations are permitted for ELLs in order to include these accommodations in ELL instruction and assessment on a regular basis. Updates to the accommodations can be found at http://pegasus. cc.ucf.edu/~fmihai/.

Alabama

Alabama has five large-scale state tests that allow accommodations for ELLs: Dynamic Indicators of Basic Early Literacy Skills; Stanford 10; the Alabama Reading and Mathematics Test; the Alabama Direct Assessment of Writing (ADAW) for Grades 5, 7, and 10; and the Alabama High School Graduation Exam (AHSGE). All five allow scheduling, setting, and format and/ or equipment accommodations. ADAW and AHSGE also allow recording accommodations.

Scheduling accommodations include flexible scheduling and shorter periods of testing with a break. Setting accommodations include flexible seating (in the ESL classroom, in a carrel), the use of an interpreter, and small-group and individual testing. Format and/or equipment accommodations include access to a translation dictionary or an electronic translator, reading aloud in English by the test administrator, noise buffers, markers to maintain one's place, and templates. Recording accommodations include allowing ELL students to mark the answers by machine (a typewriter or a word processor without a spell-checker, grammar checker, or dictionary programs) or in the test booklets.

Alaska

There are three statewide standardized tests in Alaska: the Comprehensive System of Student Assessment, the Standards-Based Assessment for Grades 3–9, and the High School Graduation Qualifying Examination. Students who are identified as LEP must participate in these academic assessments and are allowed the following test accommodations: frequent breaks during testing, additional time, flexible scheduling over several days, and individual or small-group administration. In addition, directions may be read, clarified in a student's native language, simplified, and repeated in English. Unknown words in test questions or in prompts may be provided to students in their native language if they request them. Students may also use a bilingual dictionary without pictures or definitions.

Arizona

For Grades 3–10, the state of Arizona has a statewide assessment program named Arizona's Instrument to Measure Standards—Dual-Purpose Assessment. High school students are assessed with Arizona's Instrument to Measure Standards—High School. The allowed standard accommodations fall into four categories: timing and scheduling, setting, presentation, and response. Timing and setting accommodations include extended time, breaks, and shorter sessions. Setting accommodations include small-group or individual test administration and preferential seating. Presentation accommodations include repeating, clarifying, and simplifying the directions in English; oral translation of the directions into an ELL's native language; reading the test items aloud; and access to a translation dictionary. Response accommodations include recording or dictating responses to a scribe, recording answers or typing with spell-checker and grammar checker turned off.

Arkansas

Arkansas requires the administration of criterion-referenced and norm-referenced tests. For Grades 3–8, the criterion-referenced test was combined with the Stanford Achievement Test, Tenth Edition (SAT-10), to form the Augmented Benchmark Examinations. In addition to math and literacy assessments, in Grades 5 and 7, the assessment contains a science section. In Grades 9–12, the assessment incorporates the Grade 11 Literacy Examination and End-of-Course Examinations in algebra, geometry, and biology. The accommodations for ELLs include extended time, access to a bilingual dictionary with no definitions and pictures, individualized scheduling, preferential seating, individual/small group testing, reading of the test in English, and noise buffer.

California

The state of California administers a number of tests under the Standardized Testing and Reporting program. In addition, all public school students must pass the California High School Exit Examination in order to graduate and receive a diploma. Test accommodations for ELLs include extra time, flexible scheduling, extra breaks, flexible setting, individual test administration, simplified test directions, oral translation of the test directions into a student's native language, reading the test questions aloud or presenting them by audio, access to glossaries or word lists from English to the native language without definitions or formulas, marking the answers in the test booklet, responding orally to a scribe, and access to word processing software.

Colorado

Colorado administers the Colorado Student Assessment Program, and its accommodations occur either in the presentation of the content or in the response procedures. Presentation accommodations include extended time, more frequent breaks, reading aloud the directions, and an oral presentation or translation of the entire test. Response accommodations include using a scribe for oral responses in English or the native language and utilizing assistive technology.

Connecticut

The assessment instruments used in Connecticut are the Connecticut Academic Performance Test and the Connecticut Mastery Test. The acceptable accommodations for ELLs are additional time, small-group and individualized test administration, test directions read in the native language, and the use of a dictionary with word-to-word translations without definitions.

Delaware

The state of Delaware's standardized assessment is known as the Delaware Student Testing Program (DSTP). ELLs may take the test under the following conditions: standard conditions (no accommodations for ELLs), with accommodations that permit the aggregation of test scores, or with accommodations that do not permit the aggregation of test scores. ELLs may also participate in the Delaware Alternate Portfolio Assessment, be exempted from the science and social studies test, or be granted special flexibility for the reading and writing test through an alternative assessment instead of DSTP reading and writing.

Accommodations that allow the aggregation of test scores are the following: individual or group test administration, flexible setting, flexible scheduling, extra breaks, reading and repeating the test directions in English, the use of an electronic (word-for-word translation) or bilingual dictionary, access to a bilingual (Spanish-English) version of the test or a Spanish-only version of the test, and the use of interpreters.

In addition, the responses may be written in Spanish or dictated, and the ELL's native language may be used for the first draft of the writing test. There are also accommodations that produce scores that may not be aggregated: simplifying or paraphrasing the test directions or items in English or the native language, translation by the interpreter of questions and multiple choice options into the student's native language, and translation by the interpreter of reading passages into the ELL's native language.

District of Columbia

Students in the District of Columbia must attain a level of achievement on the Stanford Achievement Test, Ninth Edition (Stanford 9), or a reading and math assessment. There are four levels of participation for ELLs on the Stanford 9 test. The decision of what level of participation a student should be placed in is made by the ESL or bilingual instructors, based on the annually administered Language Assessment Scales. The levels of participation are: Level 1, standard conditions with no accommodations; Level 2, standard conditions with special accommodations (flexible scheduling, extra breaks, small-group or individual administration, flexible seating, the repetition of directions, the simplification of oral directions); Level 3, nonstandard conditions with permissible accommodations (a separate testing site, extended time, and breaks); and Level 4, test exemption (e.g., for students with less than three years of academic instruction in English).

Florida

The statewide assessment in Florida is the Florida Comprehensive Assessment Test, and ELLs are allowed the following accommodations: additional time, flexible scheduling, flexible setting and seating, the use of a bilingual dictionary, and an explanation of the directions in the student's native language.

Georgia

The state of Georgia has several statewide assessment instruments: the Georgia High School Graduation Test, the End-of-Course Test, the Criterion-Referenced Competency Test, and others. The accommodations include extended time; multiple breaks; small-group or individual administration;

flexible setting; flexible seating; explaining, repeating, or paraphrasing the oral directions in English; reading the test in English to the students; marking the answers in the test booklet; and pointing to the answers or verbally responding (in English).

Hawaii

The standardized test in Hawaii, the Hawaii State Assessment, allows more than 20 accommodations, with the following at the top of the list: extended time, individualized administration, and the use of computers and audiotapes.

Idaho

Idaho uses the Idaho State Testing Program, and its accommodations are divided into the following categories: administration and presentation, scheduling, response, and assistive technology. Administrative and presentation accommodations include clarifying; providing written, oral, or audio-taped test directions in English or in the student's native language; reading the test items and test directions in English; prompting the students to stay focused; and allowing an English or a bilingual word-to word dictionary. Scheduling accommodations include extra time, small-group administration, and flexible scheduling. Response accommodations include the dictation of answers to a scribe in English or in the native language. Assistive technology accommodations consist of noise buffers, the use of a calculator, and special lighting.

Illinois

The two major standardized tests in Illinois are the Illinois Standards Achievement Test, administered in Grades 3, 5, and 8, and the Prairie State Achievement Examination, administered in the 11th grade. For these tests, some of the allowed accommodations for ELLs are extended time, breaks during testing, small-group or individual administration, translated test directions, the use of audiotapes, and the transcription of oral responses.

Indiana

The current standardized test in Indiana is the Indiana Statewide Testing for Educational Progress (ISTEP+). Testing accommodations are available for students whose first language is not English. These accommodations can be divided into two categories. The first is accommodations that are permitted but not documented on the ISTEP+ student information questionnaire; these include flexible scheduling, additional breaks, flexible seating, small-group or individual administration, access to large-print versions, and reading the directions to the student. The second category is accommodations that are both permitted and documented on the ISTEP+ student information questionnaire; these include extended time, oral response to the multiple choice questions or the writing section, additional examples, and reading the test questions.

Iowa

The standardized tests that Iowa uses are the Iowa Test of Basic Skills for K–8 and the Iowa Test of Educational Development for Grades 9–12. The accommodations include extra time to complete the test, the use of a translation dictionary, reading aloud parts of the test or the entire test to the student, and providing word pronunciations or definitions when such help does not interfere with the subject matter or the skills that are being tested.

Kansas

The standardized test used in Kansas is the Kansas General Assessment, and its accommodations are as follows: additional time, small-group or individual test administration, an electronic translator or a bilingual dictionary, reading aloud the directions and the test (except the reading passages) in English, and access to an online Spanish version that is read aloud to the student automatically.

Kentucky

The standardized test in Kentucky is called the Commonwealth Accountability Testing System (CATS) and includes the Kentucky Core Content Test, the Comprehensive Test of Basic Skills, and writing portfolios and prompts. Some accommodations allowed for CATS are reading the text to ELLs in English, paraphrasing the directions in English or the native language, small-group administration, alternate scheduling because of a limited number of interpreters, the use of foreign language and English dictionaries, the use of student-made glossaries, the use of a word processor and grammar checking and spell-checking, extended time, and the use of a scribe or an interpreter.

According to the Kentucky Department of Education, the purpose of these accommodations is to decrease the language demands of the test items without negatively impacting the content that is to be measured—that is, the validity of the test.

Louisiana

Louisiana administers several standardized tests, of which the Louisiana Educational Assessment Program and the Graduation Exit Examination are the most important. Accommodations for ELLs include extended time, small-group or individual administration, using a standard or an electronic bilingual dictionary without definitions, reading the test aloud, and translating the test directions into the native language of the student.

Maine

Maine administers the Maine Educational Assessment, and it has four categories of accommodations: schedule, setting, equipment, and modality. Schedule accommodations include extended time and flexible scheduling. Setting accommodations consist of small-group or individual administration, flexible setting, and flexible seating. Equipment accommodations include the use of a bilingual dictionary and the use of a typewriter or a word processor. Modality accommodations include the administrator reading the test to the student, local personnel translating the test into the ELL's native language or the student responses into English, and reading and administering the test in a "sheltered (or simplified) English" content.

Maryland

Maryland uses a test called the Maryland School Assessment. The accommodations are categorized as presentation, response, timing and scheduling, and setting. Presentation accommodations consist of reading or playing an audiotape of the entire test or sections of it, the use of a videotape test format, the use of a screen reader for the entire test or a section of it, and talking materials. Response accommodations include marking the answers on the test booklet, monitoring the test response, allowing a scribe, using an electronic note taker or a word processor, tape-recording the answers, using a spell-checker and a grammar checker, and using a bilingual dictionary. Timing and scheduling accommodations include extended time, flexible scheduling (such as multiple and frequent breaks), and changing the order of the activities on one day or on multiple days. Setting accommodations include reducing distractions to the students and creating a flexible setting.

Massachusetts

All students, including ELLs and students with disabilities, are required to take the Massachusetts Comprehensive Assessment System (MCAS). In addition, ELLs must take the Massachusetts English Proficiency Assessment to measure their annual progress in English. For the MCAS, Spanish-speaking ELLs in 10th grade who have been enrolled for less than 3 years in the continental U.S. K–12 system can take the English-Spanish version of the Grade 10 math test if they can read and write in Spanish at or near grade level. When taking the MCAS in English, ELLs are allowed to use a word-to-word bilingual dictionary without definitions, antonyms, phrases, or any other information.

Michigan

The Michigan state test is called the Michigan Educational Assessment Program, and its standard accommodations are divided into four categories: timing and scheduling, setting, presentation, and response. Timing and scheduling accommodations allow the ELLs extended time, frequent breaks, and flexible scheduling. Setting accommodations consist of flexible seating, flexible setting, small-group administration, and permission to move without distracting the other students. Presentation accommodations include the use of translation glossaries, the use of audio versions of the test, the use of video versions of the test in Arabic or in Spanish for basic or lower-intermediate English-proficient students, administration of the subtests in a flexible order, and reading the directions or the entire test in either English or the student's native language. Response accommodations include using a scribe or pointing to the answers and/or writing directly in the assessment booklet (the answers are later transferred to the answer sheet by the teacher who is administering the test).

Minnesota

Minnesota is in a transition period in testing its ELLs. The statewide standardized exam is called the Minnesota Comprehensive Assessment (MCA), but ELLs take the Test of Emerging Academic English (TEAE) instead. Other tests are being developed for the assessment of ELLs: the TEAE listening and speaking, and the TEAE in math. At this time, all testing materials, as well as the information for these materials, are available in the languages of the most predominant second-language groups in Minnesota: Spanish, Laotian, Russian, and Vietnamese. In addition, there are accommodations for ELLs who take the MCA in English: access to an English script or an audio version, the use of an English script that is orally translated into the student's native language, the use of a bilingual scribe who translates the open-ended response items, and the use of a word-to-word dictionary.

Mississippi

Mississippi administers the Mississippi Statewide Assessment System, and its accommodations fall into four categories: setting, time and scheduling, presentation, and response. Setting accommodations consist of flexible setting, flexible seating, and small-group or individual administration. Time and scheduling accommodations include flexible scheduling, additional time, and multiple breaks. Presentation accommodations include reading the test directions and items (with or without repeating and/or paraphrasing), highlighting key words in the directions, cuing the students to stay on task, and the use of memory aids, fact charts, and resource sheets. Response accommodations include dictating the answers to a scribe, marking the answers in the test booklet, and using a bilingual dictionary without definitions and/or a spelling dictionary.

Missouri

The Missouri Assessment Program is the statewide standardized test in the state of Missouri, and it allows the following accommodations: small-group or individual administration, extended time, flexible scheduling (administering the test in more than the allotted time periods), reading the test aloud in English and in the student's native language, the use of a bilingual dictionary, and the use of a scribe to record the student's oral response in the test booklet.

Montana

In Montana, students who have been identified as LEP and who have been instructed in English for more than three years take the Iowa Tests. There are several approved standard and nonstandard accommodations: small-group or individual administration; extended time; flexible scheduling; the repetition, clarification, or translation of the directions; reading the test aloud; transferring the answers from the test booklet to the answer sheets; and the use of a bilingual word-to-word dictionary and/or assistive technology.

Nebraska

Nebraska currently uses the School-Based Teacher-Led Assessment Reporting System as its instrument for statewide assessment. Standard accommodations include flexible scheduling, flexible setting, extended time, multiple breaks, a large-print version of the test, the translation of key words in the text, a bilingual version of the test, and a bilingual dictionary. The test administration may also be modified, allowing the students to dictate their responses to a scribe or record their responses on tape, to be transcribed later for scoring.

Nevada

ELLs in Nevada take the Nevada Proficiency Examination, and its accommodations fall into three categories: setting, scheduling, and administration. Setting accommodations include individual or small-group administration and alternative settings. The sole scheduling accommodation is extended time. Administration accommodations include allowing the ESL teacher to administer the test, defining the words in the writing prompts, the use of a bilingual dictionary or a word-by-word translator, answering questions about the testing procedures, and reading the directions and/or the test aloud in English.

New Hampshire

In response to the requirements of NCLB to test all students in Grades 3–8 in mathematics and reading or language arts, New Hampshire, Rhode Island, and Vermont have developed a common set of grade-level expectations known as the New England Common Assessment Program Grade-Level Expectations. The accommodations are divided into four categories: setting, time and scheduling, presentation, and response

Setting accommodations include small-group or individual test administration, flexible setting, and preferential seating. Time and scheduling accommodations include breaks and extended time. Presentation accommodations include the administrator reading the test aloud to the students, the students reading the test aloud to themselves, translating the directions into a student's native language, and the use of a word-to-word translation dictionary with no definitions. Response accommodations include using a word processor, making handwritten responses on a separate piece of paper that will be transcribed later in the answer booklet, indicating responses to the multiple choice items, and dictating responses to be recorded in the answer booklet.

New Jersey

There are several standardized tests in New Jersey. Two of the most important are the New Jersey Assessment of Skills and Knowledge (NJ ASK) and the High School Proficiency Assessment (HSPA). There are three available accommodations for NJ ASK: additional time, the translation of the test directions into the native language of the student, and the use of a bilingual translation dictionary. HSPA also provides accommodations and modifications, which include extended time, small-group administration, access to a translation dictionary, and the translation of the test directions into the student's native language.

New Mexico

The state of New Mexico administers a statewide assessment test called the New Mexico High School Competency Examination, which covers reading, language arts, science, math, social studies, and writing. It allows the following accommodations: extended time, flexible scheduling, multiple breaks, small-group or individual administration, flexible seating, flexible setting, reading and/or translating the test directions and test items, repeating the directions, access to a bilingual dictionary, and clarification of words in English.

New York

In the state of New York, ELLs must take all the required state tests and regents exams in high school. They are also required to take the New York State English as a Second Language Achievement Test. The accommodations for the latter are extra time, flexible setting, access to a bilingual dictionary and a glossary, oral translation, and writing the responses in the student's native language. For the other elementary and middle school state standardized tests and the regents exams, the accommodations are flexible setting, additional time, repeating the test items, access to a translated or bilingual version of the test in certain languages (Chinese, Haitian-Creole, Korean, Russian, and Spanish), and an oral translation of the tests in other languages.

North Carolina

The North Carolina Testing Program is administered at the end of each grade level from Grades 3 to 12. There are six testing accommodations for students identified as LEP: flexible scheduling, flexible setting (a separate room), the students reading the test aloud to themselves, the test administrator reading the test aloud in English, and access to a word-to-word bilingual dictionary or an electronic translator without definitions.

North Dakota

The North Dakota State Assessment is required for students in Grades 3–8 and 11, and it has three categories of accommodations for ELLs that determine the degree to which the intervention is required. Category 1 accommodations require the least amount of intervention and allow extra assessment. Category 2 accommodations require limited intervention and include reading the directions and the questions aloud to the students, providing the assessment in the native language of the student, and providing a general glossary and a general dictionary. Category 3 accommodations requires extensive alterations during the assessment and consists of modifications of the test directions: providing oral translations, explanations in English or the in native language of the student, and simplified instructions that clarify what a test item is asking.

Ohio

Ohio administers the Ohio Achievement Test for students in Grades 3–8, and it allows the use of a dictionary and extended time to complete the test. ELLs who have been enrolled in U.S. schools for less than three years and are at the beginning or intermediate level in reading and writing are eligible to receive one of the following three additional accommodations: an English read-aloud of allowable parts of the test, an oral translation of allowable parts of the test, or a Spanish-English bilingual printed form of the test.

Oklahoma

The Oklahoma School Testing Program consists of a norm-referenced test, represented by the Iowa Tests of Basic Skills (ITBS), and a criterion-referenced test, represented by the Oklahoma Core Curriculum Tests (OCCT). The accommodations for ITBS are listed under Iowa. For OCCT, the accommodations consist of additional time; flexible scheduling; small-group or individual administration; reading, repeating, simplifying, or clarifying the test instructions in English; oral translation of the test directions and items into the student's native language; and the transfer of the student's responses to the standard answer sheets by the test administrators.

Oregon

Oregon's standardized test is the Oregon Statewide Assessment System, and its accommodations are divided into four categories: presentation, setting, time and scheduling, and response. Presentation accommodations include explaining the directions, reading aloud the directions in English and in the student's native language, translating the directions into the student's native language, a bilingual (Spanish only) version of the test, and a bilingual dictionary without definitions. Setting accommodations consist of small-group or individual testing and flexible seating. Time and scheduling accommodations consist of extended time (on the same day), extra breaks, and extended sessions on multiple days. Response accommodations include using a scribe, writing directly in the test booklet, answering orally, and pointing to the answer.

Pennsylvania

Pennsylvania's standard test is the Pennsylvania System of School Assessment, and its assessments include the use of a word-to-word dictionary, a Spanish-English math test, and the use of a qualified interpreter to translate the directions (for math and reading) as well as words and phrases in the math section at the student's request.

Rhode Island

Like New Hampshire and Vermont, Rhode Island uses the New England Common Assessment Program to measure student achievement in reading, math, and writing in Grades 3–8. The accommodations are the same as those listed under New Hampshire.

South Carolina

There are two types of standardized tests in South Carolina, specific to grade level: the Palmetto Achievement Challenge Tests (PACT), for Grades 3–8, and the High School Assessment Program (HSAP). For PACT, the accommodations include reading the test directions and test questions aloud in English (Grade 3), administering the test on CD-ROM to students who can use computers (Grade 5 and up), and marking the answers in the test booklet. For HSAP, the accommodations consist of prior test preparation in the form of instructions that cover the test format, the directions, and test-taking strategies; access to a bilingual dictionary without pictures, definitions, or examples; rewording the directions in English or in the student's native language; small-group or individual administration; oral administration of the math section; additional time; and marking the answers in the test booklet.

South Dakota

South Dakota measures the academic achievement of its students through the Dakota State Test of Educational Progress. Its assessments are divided into four categories: scheduling, setting, presentation, and response. Scheduling accommodations include flexible scheduling and breaks between and within the subtests. Setting accommodations include small-group or individual testing and flexible setting. Presentation accommodations include repeating or simplifying the directions and reading the test questions aloud to the students. Response accommodations include the use of visual aids (templates, masks, and markers), a dictionary, a word list, and/or a glossary.

Tennessee

The state of Tennessee has a standardized assessment known as the Tennessee Comprehensive Assessment Program (TCAP) with four different tests: TCAP Achievement, TCAP Competency, TCAP Secondary Assessment, and TCAP Writing. The accommodations include extended time, the use of a bilingual dictionary, and reading the test directions and the test items aloud in English, with the exception of the language arts subtests (e.g., reading and spelling).

Texas

The standardized assessment instrument in Texas is the Texas Assessment of Knowledge and Skills (TAKS), which measures student performance in reading, writing, math, science, and social studies. Spanish-speaking students who are identified as LEP are allowed to take the test in Spanish for up to 3 years. If after 3 years the students are still not ready to take the test in English, they work with a grade-placement committee to get on track. Other accommoda-

tions include translating the directions, small-group or individual administration, and English language dictionaries.

In 2005, Texas began administering Linguistically Accommodating Testing (LAT) for students in Grades 3–10 who are exempt from TAKS because
they are classified as LEP. LAT allows for language help with the math portion
of TAKS and consists of a bilingual dictionary and reading assistance in which
the test administrators read words or sentences aloud.

Utah

To assess student academic performance statewide, Utah employs the Utah
Performance Assessment System for Students. This test has grouped its accommodations according to level of English proficiency. For pre-emergent–non-
English-proficient (NEP), students, the accommodations include small-group
or individual administration, additional breaks, audio-taped directions or a
translation of the directions in the student's native language, simplification
of the test language, and encouragement to continue. At the emergent–NEP
and LEP levels, the accommodations include all of those for the first level plus
the use of a bilingual vocabulary list. Students at the advanced-fluent level are
allowed additional rest periods, audio-taped or oral directions, simplified test
language, extra examples, and the use of a bilingual vocabulary list or a list of
math and science symbols.

Vermont

Beginning in the fall of 2005, Vermont introduced the New England Common Assessment Program, which is also used in New Hampshire and Rhode
Island. For the accommodations, see the section on New Hampshire.

Virginia

Virginia has a statewide testing program called the Standards of Learning
(SOL) assessment. Its accommodations are divided into two categories: standard accommodations, which do not change what the test is measuring, and
nonstandard accommodations, which significantly change what the test is
measuring. Standard accommodations include flexible scheduling, supplemental breaks, small-group or individual administration, flexible seating,
reading the test directions and items in English to the student, simplifying
the oral directions, and transferring the students' oral responses to the answer

sheet. Nonstandard accommodations include access to a bilingual dictionary and dictation of the writing sample in English to a scribe. Even though these accommodations do alter the validity of the test, an ELL who has passed an SOL assessment using a nonstandard accommodation is considered passed, for all purposes.

Washington

Washington uses several tests to assess students statewide: the Washington Assessment of Student Learning, the Iowa Test of Basic Skills, and the Iowa Test of Educational Development. Accommodations in scheduling, setting, and presentation are offered to a student who is enrolled in a transitional bilingual program or a migrant program and is LEP. These accommodations include extended time, flexible scheduling, assessing students in their instructional setting, reading the mathematics or science items verbatim in English, and the use of a print or an electronic dictionary in English or the student's native language.

West Virginia

West Virginia administers the West Virginia Educational Standards Test, and its accommodations include flexible scheduling, extra breaks, reading the test aloud to the students, using a bilingual dictionary or an electronic translator, paraphrasing the directions, using a scribe for responses, and using a typewriter or a word processor.

Wisconsin

The Wisconsin Student Assessment System is a standardized test that measures students' academic ability in language arts, mathematics, reading, science, and social studies. ELLs may take the test with or without accommodations or may take an alternative test. There are six categories of accommodations: assistance before the test, motivation, presentation and content, response, setting, and time and scheduling.

Assistance before the test includes teaching test-taking skills and administering practice activities. Motivational accommodations consist of providing prizes and verbal encouragement.

Presentation and content accommodations include the use of magnification devices, large-print test editions, or audio amplification devices; allowing the students to mark with a pencil as they read the test content; the use of oral or audio-taped directions; simplifying, repeating, explaining, or clarifying the directions in English or in the student's native language; reading the test items in English or in simplified English; the use of an oral or a written translation of the test items; and the use of a spelling dictionary, a bilingual word list, a word-to-word dictionary, and/or a glossary.

Response accommodations include indicating the multiple choice responses to a scribe, marking the responses in the test booklet, recording the responses on audiotape, using a computer or a word processor, responding orally or writing in the student's native language, providing an audio recording of the test items in the student's native language, and providing a bilingual or a translated test version).

Setting accommodations include small-group or individual administration, flexible setting, flexible seating, and freedom of movement (standing or pacing during an individual administration). Time and scheduling accommodations involve flexible scheduling, extra time, and multiple breaks.

Wyoming

The assessment system used in Wyoming is called the Proficiency Assessment for Wyoming Students. It provides accommodations for an ELL for 3 consecutive years, beginning with the first year in which the student is enrolled. These accommodations include small-group or individual administration, the use of a translation dictionary, flexible scheduling (taking the test over several days in shorter segments), flexible setting, simplified or translated directions, clarification of words at the student's request (in English and the native language), and reading aloud the math portion of the test in English or in the student's primary language.

The Classification of State Accommodations for English Language Learners

As noted earlier, Butler and Stevens (1997) separated accommodations into two major categories, Koenig and Bachman (2004) separated them into four categories, and Pappamihiel and Mihai (2010) proposed a six-category system. Table 11 lists the accommodations according to the six-category system and summarizes their frequency of use by the states.

Table 12 lists the five most commonly used test modifications when nonnative English speakers take statewide content area tests. Four of the six-category-system elements are represented. It is not surprising to see that the most popular accommodations also require the least administrative expense, thus being very practical—but are they effective?

Table 11.   List of Accommodations and Their Frequency of Use

Category	Accommodation	Number of States Implementing It
Time and Scheduling	Additional time	39
	Flexible scheduling	28
	Extra breaks	24
Location	Individual or small-group administration	34
	Flexible setting	21
	Flexible seating	17
	Students can move around	2
Directions	Directions on audiotape in English	2
	Directions read in English	15
	Directions repeated in English	13
	Directions clarified in English	5
	Directions explained in English	3
	Directions paraphrased in English	4
	Directions simplified in English	10
	Directions rephrased in English	1
	Written version of oral directions in English or the native language	1
	Words in directions highlighted in English or the native language	1
	Directions read in the native language	4
	Directions written in the native language	1
	Directions translated into the native language (in writing)	9
	Directions translated into the native language (orally)	7
	Directions explained in the native language	2
	Directions repeated in the native language	2
	Directions clarified in the native language	2
	Directions simplified in the native language	2
	Directions paraphrased in the native language	2
	Instructions simplified in English or the native language	1
Presentation	Native-language version of test	8
	Bilingual version of test	7
	Clarification of words in English or the native language at the student's request	2
	Test questions read aloud in English	8
	Test items read in simplified English	2
	Test read aloud in English	25
	Language of test simplified	1
	Oral test administered	1
	Test items repeated in English	1
	Oral translation of words or phrases on test	1
	Test read aloud by student to self in English	5
	Test read or administered in sheltered English	1
	Oral translation of test in the native language	8
	Written translation of test items	1

Category	Accommodation	Number of States Implementing It
Presentation (*continued*)	Test read aloud in the native language	3
	Audio recording of test questions in English	5
	Audio recording of test questions in the native language	2
	Video version of test in the native language	1
	Unknown words in test questions provided in the native language	1
	Large-print version of test	3
	Additional examples	2
	Provide word pronunciation or meaning	1
	Words in writing prompts defined	1
	Translation of key words in test	1
Support	Spelling dictionary	2
	English language dictionary	1
	General dictionary	2
	Translation or bilingual dictionary	21
	Bilingual dictionary without pictures or definitions	13
	Electronic translation dictionary	6
	Electronic or print dictionary in English or the native language	1
	English or native-language glossary with no definitions	1
	Translation glossary	2
	Student-made glossary	1
	General glossary	3
	Word list	1
	English or native-language word list with no definitions	1
	Bilingual vocabulary list	2
	Typewriter or computer, no spell-checker	4
	Word processor	7
	Computer, with spell-checker	2
	Marker	1
	Noise buffer	2
	Assistive technology	5
Response	Dictating responses to scribe or teacher in English	17
	Pointing to responses	6
	Dictating responses to scribe in the native language	6
	Recording oral responses to be transcribed later in English	4
	Writing responses in test booklet	11
	Writing responses in native language	2
	Using the native language for first draft in writing	1
	Indicating responses on a separate sheet of paper to be recorded later	3
	Transferring responses to standard answer sheet	1

Table 12.   The Five Most Popular Accommodations

Accommodation	Category	Number of States Using It
Additional time	Time and scheduling	39
Use of a dictionary	Support	38
Individual or small-group administration	Location	34
Flexible scheduling	Time and scheduling	28
Test read aloud in English	Presentation	25

The Effectiveness of Large-Scale Accommodations for English Language Learners

Giving ELLs more time to take standardized state tests is the most popular accommodation implemented in the U.S. K–12 environment. Without a doubt, this accommodation is the most practical. However, accommodations must be effective or else they do not serve the purpose they were designed to serve.

In order to be effective, an accommodation should level the playing field for ELLs so that content, not language proficiency, is assessed (Abedi, Hofstetter, and Lord, 2004). Therefore, for content area tests specifically, the accommodations in large-scale assessments are designed to test constructs and academic knowledge rather than knowledge of the English language.

Research on accommodations has looked at how they have affected the test performance of students who are ELLs. Studies have compared the scores of ELLs from accommodated and un-accommodated test administrations in an effort to make sure that the validity of the test has been preserved. Unfortunately, according to Sireci, Li, and Scarpati (2003), very little research has been conducted on the effects of accommodations on the actual test performance of nonnative English speakers, on the adequacy of translating the tests into the native language of an ELL, or on whether the constructs that are being tested on an accommodated test are similar to those on the un-accommodated version of the test.

Sireci, Li, and Scarpati (2003) and Francis et al. (2006) survey the most relevant studies on the effectiveness of test accommodations as reflected by ELLs' performance on large-scale assessments. These studies can be divided into two categories: those that analyze the effectiveness of direct linguistic support, and those that analyze the effectiveness of indirect linguistic support.

This new taxonomy of accommodations—direct linguistic support and indirect linguistic support—has been proposed by Francis et al. (2006) in order to emphasize the importance of language in testing ELLs, especially on standardized assessments in the content areas. Examples of direct linguistic support are the accommodations in Table 11 in the categories of directions, presentation, support, and response; examples of indirect linguistic support are the accommodations in the categories of time and scheduling and location.

The studies selected for analysis here examine both direct and indirect linguistic support accommodations; however, a great number of research projects have focused their attention on direct linguistic accommodations.

Accommodations and Large-Scale Math Assessments

The main accommodations used in large-scale math assessments are access to a dictionary or a glossary, language simplification, use of the native language, and additional time.

Access to a Dictionary or a Glossary

Access to a dictionary or a glossary (defined as a list of definitions for selected words, terms, or phrases in a text) during a standardized large-scale test is the second most frequent accommodation (used by 38 states) for ELLs. Several studies have looked at how this accommodation translates into ELL scores.

Abedi, Courtney, and Leon (2003) focused on accommodations that are effective, valid, and feasible. For effectiveness, they compared the scores of 607 fourth grade students (of whom 279 were ELLs) and 542 eighth grade students (of whom 256 were ELLs) on a standardized math assessment. The direct linguistic support accommodations that they tested were a customized English dictionary and a computer test with a pop-up glossary (which can be defined as notes, usually made in the margins or at the end of a text, in which a word or a phrase is explained or paraphrased). The indirect linguistic support accommodations that they tested were additional time and small-group administration. The fourth grade students were given an un-accommodated version of the test as well as the accommodated version with the four accommodations mentioned. The eighth grade students were tested under standard conditions (the un-accommodated version of the test) and with two of the four accommodations: the customized dictionary and the computer test with the pop-up glossary.

The fourth grade ELLs who had access to the computer test and additional time scored significantly higher than the ELLs who took the un-accommodated version of the math test. The eighth grade ELLs who had access to the computer test scored significantly higher than the ELLs who either used the customized dictionary or took the test under standard conditions. Another important finding revealed that at both grade levels, native English speakers did not perform significantly better with any of the four accommodations than they did on the un-accommodated version. This is very strong evidence for the validity of such accommodations, which are supposed to level the playing field for ELLs and not give them an unfair advantage over their non-ELL peers.

Abedi et al. (2001) focused on the effect of access to a glossary, along with five other accommodations, on the results of a standardized math test that was administered to 950 students. The students who participated in the study fell into three categories: LEP, non-LEP, and former LEP students who had become fully proficient in English. The results showed that the gains for the LEP group were very small with access to a glossary alone, but there were improvements when the students were given additional time as well as access to a glossary.

Kiplinger, Haug, and Abedi (2000) administered items selected from the National Assessment of Educational Progress (NAEP) to fourth graders in Colorado. The NAEP test items used by the researchers were aligned with the math state assessment for Grade 4. There were 1,198 students in the study, of whom 152 were identified as ELLs. Two accommodations were employed in modifying the math test, one of which was to give the students access to an English glossary that contained definitions of non-technical words. The study found that for this accommodation, the scores of the ELL students did not improve significantly, compared to the non-ELLs. In fact, all the students scored better when they took the accommodated test. The glossary accommodation generated the most gain in scores for the ELLs, although the gain was insignificant from a statistical point of view.

Language Simplification

Although language simplification is not a very popular accommodation among the states, there has been some research on whether this is an effective test modification for ELLs. Abedi et al. (2006) administered an accommodated version of a math test to 2,321 eighth grade students. Language simplification did not have a statistically significant impact on the ELL scores. In addition, this research revealed that the language modification could not be applied to some math items because of their lack of English language complexity. However, the test did contain nine math items that were modified considerably. The scores achieved by ELLs and non-ELLs showed that both groups benefited from this accommodation, thus raising a serious concern about its validity.

NAEP math items were used by Hofstetter (2003) to look at the influence of accommodation on the test scores of Latino students. The sample consisted of 849 eighth grade students, of whom 676 were nonnative English speakers. When the students were given a linguistically simplified test booklet, the analysis of their scores showed a slightly higher performance for both ELLs and non-ELLs, compared to their peers who received the standard, un-accommodated version of the test. This finding raises a serious concern about the validity of this accommodation.

Another study that looked at language simplification was conducted by Abedi, Hofstetter, et al. (2001). For the 950 eighth graders who participated, it was found that modified English was the only accommodation that proved to be effective, out of five types studied, in reducing the score differences between the LEP and non-LEP students. The authors cautioned that the gap reduction between the two sets of scores was because the non-LEP students performed poorest on this version of the test, not because the LEP students scored significantly better on this version.

Language simplification was the focus of two other studies (Abedi et al., 1997; Abedi & Lord, 2001). In both studies, the researchers used 20 simplified eighth grade math items and administered both the standard and the simplified items to more than 1,000 students, of whom 30% were classified as ELLs. The findings revealed that this accommodation was beneficial not only for ELLs in the lowest level mathematics classes but also for the native English speakers who were designated as low socioeconomic status (SES). Therefore, the researchers concluded that certain language features, such as passive verb structures and unknown words, contributed to the difficulty of text interpretation for both ELL and non-ELL students in the lowest level of math classes.

Investigating the effectiveness of the same type of accommodation, Kiplinger, Haug, and Abedi (2000) found that there was no significant difference between the scores of ELLs and those of non-ELLs when they took a fourth grade standardized assessment with and without language simplification. The researchers also concluded that because all students did achieve higher scores, such an accommodation might benefit all students, not just ELLs.

Abedi, Lord, and Hofstetter (1998) found that math tests with modified English helped ELLs to achieve scores that were comparable with the scores achieved by non-ELLs. The sample in this study consisted of 1,394 eighth grade students, of whom 864 were classified as ELLs. ELLs scored higher on the simplified-English version of the test than on the standard, unmodified version. However, non-ELLs scored higher than ELLs when they were given the same accommodation, thus raising a question about the validity of this accommodation.

Use of Native Language

Another accommodation of direct linguistic support is the use of an ELL's native language. Abedi et al. (2006) looked at the scores of more than 2,000 eighth graders who took a standardized math test. They found no significant results for ELLs who took the dual-language (English and Spanish) version of the math assessment. The ELL students who were given this accommodation performed the same as the ELLs who took the un-accommodated version of the test.

Hofstetter (2003) also investigated the issue of using an ELL's native language as an effective and appropriate accommodation. This research brought to light a very interesting finding: Under certain conditions, the students who received the Spanish translation of a math test tended to perform *lower* than the students who did not receive this accommodation! For students who had been instructed in English, the Spanish-translated test had a negative, though not statistically significant, influence on their scores. However, for students who had been instructed in Spanish, the Spanish-translated test helped; their performance was better than that of the students who received no accommodation. This research suggests that native-language translation of a test helps ELLs only when the ELLs have been instructed in that language.

Garcia et al. (2000) also looked at the effectiveness of test translation. The test they used was a dual-language booklet in which math items in English and Spanish were placed side by side. The 402 eighth graders who participated in the study were divided into three groups: ELLs who received three years of academic instruction in English, ELLs who received less than three years of academic instruction in English, and non-ELLs. The ELLs who were less proficient in English performed better on the dual-language version of the test. However, the ELLs with more than three years of instruction in English performed slightly worse on the bilingual version than the ELLs who were administered the English-only version of the test. Clearly, this finding suggests that extended instruction in English was a determining factor in the performance of ELLs.

A somewhat similar finding was presented by Abedi et al. (1998). The students were randomly selected and assigned one of three versions of the test: a standard version with no modifications, a language-simplified version, and a version translated into the native language of the students, which was Spanish. The ELL students scored the highest when they took the modified-English version, and they scored the lowest when they took the Spanish-translation version. This result is consistent with the findings of both Hofstetter (2003) and Garcia et al. (2000) on Spanish-translation effectiveness.

Additional Time

Allowing ELLs to have additional time when they take a standardized state test is the most common accommodation (implemented in almost 80% of the states). Abedi, Courtney, and Leon (2003) found that ELLs who received extra time had significantly higher scores than the students who were not given this accommodation. However, in an earlier study, Abedi, Hofstetter, et al. (2001) had found that ELL scores *did* improve under this specific accommodation but that the gains for ELLs were very small.

Hafner (2000) also researched the effectiveness of additional time for ELLs who were taking standardized math tests. The study examined the effects of providing additional time and extended oral presentations of the directions and the test items (simplifying, rereading, giving additional examples). The assessment instrument was the TerraNova math test, developed by CTB/McGraw-Hill (available at www.ctb.com). The sample consisted of 451 participants who were fourth and seventh grade students from California and New Mexico. The study showed that both accommodations improved ELLs and non-ELLs' scores compared to the scores of students taking the test under standard conditions. From a statistical point of view, though, only giving the students more time significantly increased ELL and non-ELL scores.

Accommodations and Large-Scale Science Assessments

The research on test accommodations on standardized science tests is not as extensive as the research on math test accommodations. The studies in this area have focused on two accommodations: access to a dictionary or a glossary and English language simplification.

Abedi, Leon, and Mirocha (2001) investigated the use of a dictionary or a glossary with a 20-item NAEP science test that was administered to 422 eighth grade students, of whom 183 were identified as ELLs. The researchers wanted to evaluate two test versions: a test with a customized English dictionary that included only the words on the science test and a test with English and Spanish glossaries, which were explanatory notes in the margins that identified and explained key terms on the test.

The scores indicated that the ELLs' performance was the best when they took the test with the customized dictionary, whereas their performance on the test with the glossaries was similar to their performance on the standard, un-accommodated test. A very important finding was that there were no significant differences in the test scores of non-ELL students, regardless of which test they took; this is a positive indicator of construct validity.

Abedi, et al. (2005) looked at the performance of 611 fourth and eighth grade students on a science test based on released NAEP test items. Of the 611 participants, 52% were classified as ELLs. The test was administered with three accommodations: access to an English dictionary, access to a bilingual dictionary, and language simplification of the test content.

The mean score for the fourth grade ELLs who had access to an English dictionary was significantly higher than the mean score for the fourth grade ELLs who took the test with no accommodations. The eighth grade ELLs who had access to an English dictionary did not show a statistically significant increase in their mean score compared to that of the standard-condition ELL group.

The fourth grade ELL students who were provided with a bilingual dictionary performed significantly higher than the ELLs who took the test under standard conditions. Once again, there was no significant difference between the eighth grade groups.

The third accommodation, language simplification of the test content, was defined as modifications that made the English vocabulary more accessible to ELLs and the syntax less complex without reducing the complexity of the science content of the test. The fourth grade ELLs who received this accommodation did not score significantly better than their ELL peers who took the un-accommodated test. However, the eighth grade ELLs who were given the linguistic modifications did outperform their ELL peers who took the un-accommodated test.

These results suggested that the effectiveness of accommodations may vary among grade levels. The English dictionary was the most effective accommodation for Grade 4, whereas the language simplification seemed to be the most effective accommodation for Grade 8. In addition, the validity of the assessment instrument was not affected because the three accommodations had an impact only on ELL scores and did not influence the scores of the non-ELL students.

Rivera and Stansfield (2004) looked at the differences in scores between a standard and a linguistically modified version of a science test. There were eight groups of fourth and sixth graders in the study—over 1400 non-ELLs and 109 ELLs. Because of the small sample of ELLs, the findings could not be generalized. In spite of this shortcoming, the researchers did find that for non-ELLs, linguistically simplified items are generally of very little help. A comparison of the scores of non-ELLs who took the test with accommodations and the scores of those who took the test under normal conditions showed no statistical difference. Therefore, this test accommodation does not pose a threat to the validity of the measuring instrument.

Accommodations and Large-Scale Social Science Assessments

The research on the effectiveness of ELL accommodations for social science tests is even more limited than the research on science-test accommodations. One study (Castellon-Wellington, 2000) stands out. It gathered data from a sample of 106 ELLs who took the seventh grade Iowa Test of Basic Skills (ITBS). The two accommodations that were provided for ELLs were additional time and oral repetition, or reading aloud of the text; there was no modification of the language of the test at all. The data collected indicated no difference between the scores from the accommodated and the un-accommodated tests.

Conclusions about Accommodation Research

From this review of the relevant literature on accommodation effectiveness for math, science, and social science tests, there are several conclusions that can be drawn.

First, the findings are mixed and present conflicting results. For example, some of the studies found a significant gain in scores for ELLs who took a standardized math assessment with a language-simplification accommodation; others identified a gain in ELL scores, but without statistical significance.

Second, each accommodation must be studied in isolation, not in clusters. An example is additional time; the effects of this accommodation on ELL scores are not very clear, mostly because it has been clustered with other accommodations, such as access to a dictionary or a glossary or a linguistic modification. However, when ELLs were allowed additional time to take content area standardized tests, they typically scored better than their peers who took the test under standard conditions.

Third, one accommodation does not fit all ELL students. The findings of Abedi et al. (2005) indicate that an accommodation that significantly increases the scores of ELLs at one grade level does not necessarily do so for ELLs at a different grade level.

Finally, there is a need for more research, not only on the accommodations that have already been researched but also on the entire spectrum of accommodations, especially for content area assessments. Education practitioners and researchers will have to focus much more energy in this area to identify what works best for ELLs.

An example in which research has informed the practice of ELL accommodation is the language support provided to ELLs in large-scale assessments. Dictionaries and glossaries seem to have a much more positive impact on ELL scores than test translation does; there is very little evidence of the effectiveness of dual-language test booklets.

Another critical issue that research has addressed is test validity. Some research found that non-ELL scores were not affected by accommodations, whereas other research revealed that all students benefited from an accommodation. Therefore, the very important question on which research should focus is whether specific ELL accommodations have an impact on the construct that is being tested. However, a different question is equally important: Are the scores collected through this standardized measurement valid? In other words, are high-stakes tests valid for the ELL student population?

Table 13 summarizes the research findings discussed in this section.

The Validity of Large-Scale Content Area Assessments for the English Language Learner Student Population

Current educational legislation requires that all students meet the academic standards described in their state's curriculum policies. In addition, schools are held for accountable for the progress of their students, including students who are learning English and academic content at the same time. In theory, this idea of high standards for all students sounds promising for ELLs, who were an invisible population for many years. With the educational laws in place at this time, it is assumed that more resources will be directed toward the improvement of the academic performance of ELLs and other student populations that have been overlooked in the past.

However, very important decisions on resources allocation are made by taking into account only the results of standardized large-scale achievement tests. Many states link teacher bonuses to students' test performance. Furthermore, the results of standardized achievement tests are used by many states for decisions on graduation or promotion. Given the importance that standardized assessments hold, the issue is how valid these instruments really are in gathering information on the ability of ELLs to express their knowledge in English.

Abella et al. (2005) looked at the validity of English language assessment instruments in their study, which employed more than 1,700 participants. Their research addressed three major questions.

First, the study looked at the impact of the English proficiency of ELLs on the validity of their achievement test results. Previous research in this area

Table 13.   Summary of Research on Accommodation Effectiveness

Content Area	Accommodation Type	Accommodation Category	Study: Findings
Math	Dictionary or glossary	Direct linguistic support	Abedi et al. (2003): significantly higher scores. Abedi, Hofstetter, et al. (2001): no significant gains. Kiplinger et al. (2000): no significant difference in performance.
Math	Language simplification	Direct linguistic support	Abedi et al. (2006): no significant impact on scores. Hofstetter (2003): slightly higher performance. Abedi, Hofstetter, et al. (2001): improvement in scores, small gains. Abedi & Lord (2001): beneficial for lowest-level math students. Kiplinger et al. (2000): no significant difference in performance. Abedi et al. (1998): better scores. Abedi, Lord, & Plummer (1997): beneficial for lowest-level math students.
Math	Native language	Direct linguistic support	Abedi et al. (2006): no significant impact on scores. Hofstetter (2003): higher scores under certain conditions. Garcia et al. (2000): higher scores under certain conditions. Abedi et al. (1998): lower scores.
Math	Additional time	Indirect linguistic support	Abedi et al. (2003): significantly higher scores. Abedi, Hofstetter, et al. (2001): small gains. Hafner (2000): significant increase.
Science	Dictionary or glossary	Direct linguistic support	Abedi et al. (2005): significantly higher scores depending on grade level. Abedi, Leon, & Mirocha (2001): significantly better with dictionary, minimal benefit from glossary
Science	Language simplification	Direct linguistic support	Abedi et al. (2005): significantly higher scores depending on grade level. Rivera & Stansfield (2004): no relevance.
Social science	Reading aloud	Direct linguistic support	Castellon-Wellington (2000): no score gain.
Social science	Additional time	Indirect linguistic support	Castellon-Wellington (2000): no score gain.

showed that ELLs produced invalid test results on content area tests (Abedi, Leon, & Mirocha, 2001), so there was a need to determine the effect of language proficiency on test scores.

Second, Abella et al. (2005) focused on the influence of ELLs' native-language literacy on standardized test scores. Earlier research looked at the relationship between the amount of education that ELLs have received in their native language (as well as their native-language proficiency) and their school performance (Thomas & Collier, 1997), but it had not examined the relationship between the students' educational and language-proficiency backgrounds and the validity of their test scores.

The third focus of Abella et al. (2005) is probably the most interesting. The researchers looked at the validity of the results produced by former ELLs, who after usually three years in an ESL program were mainstreamed and classified as fully proficient in English. Their scores on achievement tests were combined with the scores of the native English-speaking population.

An analysis of the results produced some very important findings. The achievement test results of ELLs generally revealed that English-based instruments were not always valid assessments of ELLs' actual content area knowledge. ELLs did better on a native-language math test than on an English language one, regardless of their level of language proficiency or their grade level.

This somewhat contradicts previous research that had found little support for the effectiveness of dual-language test booklets. Moreover, Mahon (2006) found that English language proficiency was significantly related to English academic achievement for elementary schoolchildren who were native Spanish speakers and even for ELLs who had been in a U.S. educational environment for more than three years. The need for additional research in this critical area is quite obvious.

Another finding of Abella et al. (2005) was that former ELLs who were now considered fluent speakers of English were often unable to demonstrate their content area knowledge if the test was in English. This finding is extremely important because these students were considered to have overcome the language barrier in accessing English language content. Their achievement scores were considered to be valid and were most likely used to determine whether they had made adequate yearly progress (AYP), as defined by NCLB. AYP is a very important provision of the law; it determines that a school should be subjected to restructuring if its students do not show academic progress. The fact that former ELLs cannot unequivocally show the actual level of their knowledge base in the content areas due to language and cultural difficulties is a clear indicator that these students do not compete on a level playing field with their native English-speaking peers.

The study raises serious concerns about the validity of scores collected though English language content area achievement tests. According to the authors, there was a direct connection between the validity of the scores of the ELL students and their language and educational backgrounds: the longer the ELL's education in the his or her native language, the more compromised the validity of the English language instrument. Mahon (2006) found something similar: Achievement in the native language of Spanish-speaking ELLs predicted English achievement, especially when it was combined with the English proficiency of ELLs.

Recommendations for Improving the Quality of Large-Scale Assessment Instruments

What, then, are the best ways to measure academic progress for ELLs, in light of the AYP requirements of NCLB? Perhaps the best route is to be proactive and look at what can be changed in the process of designing large-scale assessments and in the policies and procedures of standardized tests.

Test-Design Recommendations

When designing standardized large-scale achievement tests, test makers should follow the Standards for Educational and Psychological Testing, a set of standards put together by the American Psychological Association (APA), the American Educational Research Association (AERA), and the National Council on Measurement in Education (NCME) to ensure the validity and reliability of test scores. These standards include a section on testing students of diverse linguistic backgrounds.

Rhodes, Ochoa, and Ortiz (2005) summarize the six most recommended standards to be followed when creating large-scale assessments and taking ELLs into consideration. They are:

1. Language-difference threats to the reliability and the validity of test scores should be minimized as much as possible.

2. Language proficiency should be determined first so that the test can be administered in the test taker's most proficient language—especially in a content area such as math or science, in which language proficiency is not supposed to be part of the assessment.

3. Accommodations that focus on language modifications should be described in detail in the test manual and the instructions if they have been recommended and approved by the test publishers.

4. The test publishers should provide score-interpretation tables for ELLs when a test is recommended for use with linguistically diverse students.

5. When a test is translated into the native language of the ELLs, the test publishers should provide a description of the methods used to establish the adequacy of the translation, as well as evidence of validity and reliability.

6. When language interpreters are used as a testing accommodation, they should be fluent in both the language of the test and the language of the test takers, they should have expertise in translating, and they should have a basic understanding of the process.

Although these recommendations seem to fully consider the needs of ELLs, they do not sufficiently emphasize that ELLs must be considered before and during the design process and not after, as is often the case. A much better approach, which would potentially help to generate more valid and reliable scores for ELLs on large-scale assessments, is universal test design.

According to Dolan and Hall (2001), the concept of universal design originated in architecture as a way to create structures that would accommodate the largest range of users. Instead of adding ramps and elevators to an existing building for increased accessibility, for instance, universal design considers the needs of all possible building users from the very beginning. Consequently, architects can integrate universal accessibility into their design before the building is actually constructed.

Universal test design (UTD) means that assessments are designed from the start to be accessible to and valid for the widest range of students, including ELLs and students with disabilities. Instead of designing a test first and thinking of how to accommodate diverse learners after the fact, in UTD the entire testing population is considered at the outset and throughout the entire time that the test is being developed and fine-tuned.

UTD has a very important role in all aspects of assessment development. When an assessment is at the conceptual phase, UTD helps by defining the constructs in a very explicit manner and by including all students fully, regardless of their level of language proficiency. When an assessment moves to the construction phase, UTD helps in developing test items that maximize the testing of content and minimize the testing of language ability. After the try-out phase, UTD plays a critical role in item analysis and revision so that items that show different scores for different student populations can be evaluated and eliminated.

The Center for Universal Design (1997) has published seven principles of universal design, as shown in Table 14.

Table 14.   The Seven Principles of Universal Design

Principle	Definition	Guidelines
Equitable Use	The design is useful and marketable to people with diverse abilities.	• Provide the same means of use for all users: identical whenever possible, equivalent when not. • Avoid segregating or stigmatizing any users. • Provide equal privacy, security, and safety to all users. • Make the design appealing to all users.
Flexibility in Use	The design accommodates a wide range of individual preferences and abilities.	• Provide choice in the methods of use. • Accommodate right- or left-handed access and use. • Facilitate the user's accuracy and precision. • Provide adaptability to the user's pace.
Simple and Intuitive Use	The use of the design is easy to understand, regardless of the user's experience, knowledge, language skills, or current concentration level.	• Eliminate unnecessary complexity. • Be consistent with user expectations and intuition. • Accommodate a wide range of literacy and language skills. • Arrange information consistent with its importance. • Provide effective prompting and feedback during and after task completion.
Perceptible Information	The design communicates necessary information effectively to the user, regardless of ambient conditions or the user's sensory abilities.	• Use different modes (pictorial, verbal, tactile) for redundant presentation of essential information. • Provide an adequate contrast between essential information and its surroundings. • Maximize the legibility of essential information. • Differentiate elements in ways that can be described (i.e., make it easy to give instructions or directions). • Provide compatibility with a variety of techniques or devices used by people with sensory limitations.
Tolerance for Error	The design minimizes hazards and the adverse consequences of accidental or unintended actions.	• Arrange elements to minimize hazards and errors: most used elements are the most accessible; hazardous elements are eliminated, isolated, or shielded. • Provide warnings of hazards and errors. • Provide fail-safe features. • Discourage unconscious action in tasks that require vigilance.
Low Physical Effort	The design can be used efficiently and comfortably and with a minimum of fatigue.	• Allow the user to maintain a neutral body position. • Use reasonable operating procedures. • Minimize repetitive actions. • Minimize sustained physical effort.
Size and Space for Approach and Use	Appropriate size and space is provided for approach, reach, manipulation, and use, regardless of the user's body size, posture, or mobility.	• Provide a clear line of sight to important elements for any seated or standing user. • Make the reach to all components comfortable for any seated or standing user. • Accommodate variations in hand and grip size. • Provide adequate space for assistive devices or personal assistance.

Dolan and Hall (2001) identify three ways in which the principle of universal design can be applied to the construction of large-scale assessments: through multiple means of recognition, expression, and engagement.

First, the students should be provided with multiple means of recognition. In order to provide basic access to ELLs who are identified as LEP and multiple routes to meaning for all students, large-scale content area assessments should provide multiple representations of meaning. For example, if the construct to be assessed during a math test is the principle of mathematic probability, representing the questions both as word problems and using graphics may generate more valid and reliable scores not only for ELLs but also for the entire student population.

Second, the test takers should be provided with multiple means of expression. Writing, a difficult task for many ELLs, continues to be the principal method of expression on standardized tests. When writing ability in itself represents a barrier to the accurate measure of an ELL's ability in a content area, alternative means of expression should be considered. For ELLs who have low English language proficiency in writing, speech-to-text technology or the use of a scribe can constitute valid substitutes for the more traditional forms of answering test items.

Third, students should be provided with multiple means of engagement. It is well known that tests induce anxiety in students, thus negatively affecting the reliability of the scores. One way of improving the engagement of students during tests is to provide them with choices. In social studies, ELLs can choose test tasks based on their particular interests, which could improve their engagement. Tests can also go beyond the practical, yet not very engaging, text-based format by implementing digital manipulatives that contribute positively to students' engagement.

When test designers apply universal design principles during assessment construction, they are more likely to create tests that assess the knowledge and abilities of all student populations. Because these principles call for the consideration of ELLs' language abilities, they reduce the need for many of the accommodations that are used today as post-design modifications.

Policy Recommendations

The six categories of accommodations (Pappamihiel & Mihai, 2010) that were shown in Table 11 are the most frequent descriptors found on state testing websites, and on the surface they seem to be quite consistent. However, when these categories are examined in more detail, it is evident that the implementation of the accommodations is quite varied and could impact the validity and comparison of the test scores in many ways.

For example, there are 20 possible accommodations that involve testing support, which can be further divided into two subcategories. The first subcategory targets the reduction of the linguistic burden, whereas the second one aims at increasing focus. In the first subcategory, the most widespread type of accommodation is allowing the use of a dictionary. However, there are critical differences among the states. For example, some states allow a bilingual dictionary, whereas others (Arkansas and Massachusetts) allow such a dictionary, but without definitions or pictures. Some states (Wisconsin and Mississippi) allow a spelling dictionary, whereas others firmly forbid them.

This inconsistency in policy is well illustrated by the state of Texas. Texas policy allows the use of an English language dictionary but does not recommend a specific type of dictionary. Dictionaries are quite varied in type (print or electronic), language (bilingual or monolingual), and usage (translation or definition). As a result, this level of generalization is unacceptable because each dictionary-based accommodation could have a different impact on reducing the linguistic burden and may pose a threat to the validity of content area test scores for ELLs.

This brief examination of accommodation policies reveals that there is little consistency among the states on testing accommodations for ELLs. This inconsistency could be related to the lack of information on the effectiveness of testing accommodations for ELLs. Although most of the accommodations for ELLs are modeled on the testing accommodations made for students with disabilities (Zehr, 2006), which have a much longer history, it is clear that ELLs and students with disabilities face dramatically different issues when taking large-scale assessments.

The states obviously use accommodations to level the playing field for ELLs in high-stakes testing programs to increase the validity of the test scores. Yet as we have discussed, the actual validity of these accommodations is in serious question.

According to NCLB, the states are required to make valid instruments to measure content growth and, for ELLs, language proficiency. Although many states are making progress in measuring English proficiency, the U.S. Department of Education is taking the lead in helping the states to develop guiding standards so that we can all be consistent in our use of English proficiency standards. There is an evident need for a similar consistency in providing accommodations when we test ELLs in the academic content areas. Without this careful consideration, we face the possibility of once again invalidating the test results of ELLs and blaming the students for the failures of a broken system.

In summary, a detailed examination of content area test accommodations for ELLs has revealed that there is still a lot to be done in order to have an accurate measure of the knowledge base of this student population. The research on the effectiveness of ELL test accommodation is, quite surprisingly, rather limited, despite the fact that the test scores that are obtained through these measurements are extremely important for students, teachers, parents, and school administrators. The signs are encouraging, however. Educational legislation at the state and federal level requires that ELLs be tested in a valid and reliable manner, and more states want to ensure the validity and reliability of their test scores. Universal Test Design might prove to be a very valuable tool in the near future of test development.

Things to Consider

- The most common large-scale test accommodations for ELLs include giving ELLs additional time to take the test, allowing them to use a dictionary or glossary, and administering the assessment individually or in small groups.

- Accommodations are not automatically provided to ELLs even when students are identified as not being fully proficient in English.

- Content area teachers should familiarize themselves with accommodations that are sanctioned by the state in which they are teaching to include them in instruction and class-room-based assessment.

- From the available set of accommodation, content area teachers should emphasize the accommodations that directly address the language needs of ELLs to make tests a valid measure of academic knowledge and not one of English proficiency.

- The choice allowing ELLs to take bilingual or native language forms of large-scale assessments must take into account the ELLs' proficiency in their native language, as well as the language in which they have been instructed.

Chapter 4

Classroom-Based Assessment in the Content Areas and English Language Learners

This chapter will discuss what classroom teachers can do to create accurate assessment tools for their ELL students. It will examine several critical issues related to language proficiency in the content areas, and it will provide classroom teachers in the content areas with useful tools for designing assessments that subscribe to all the principles of assessment: validity, reliability, practicality, equivalency, and wash-back.

An important characteristic of the contemporary educational environment in the United States is the development of comprehensive standards of achievement that are used by educational entities and stakeholders, with two purposes in mind. First, these standards of achievement are the foundation on which curriculum developers build a statewide curriculum, which in turn is the basis for classroom instruction and materials (i.e., textbooks and other teaching materials). Second, and more important from an assessment perspective, these academic standards are used as the most important criteria for measuring student achievement through classroom-based and large-scale assessments.

The creation of these standards of achievement has been seen as a response to the need to provide consistency and accountability for the content that is taught in K–12 classrooms in the United States. Students should get quality instruction regardless of teaching style, location, or student characteristics such as demographics, socioeconomic status, or English language proficiency. Today, as a result of legislative initiatives such as No Child Left Behind (NCLB), teachers are held accountable for the academic progress and achievement of *all* of their students, including students whose native language is not English. Therefore, content area teachers should and must take into consideration the needs of this student population, in light of the phenomenal growth in the number of ELLs in the past decade.

The Importance of Assessing English Language Learners in Content Area Classrooms

O'Malley and Pierce (1996) identify three reasons that content area assessments are vital for ELLs and their content area instructors: monitoring, reclassification, and accountability.

First, content area teachers can monitor their ELLs' progress in achieving the instructional objectives that have been set by the curriculum standards to determine if their instruction is effective. If the instructional objectives are not being met and ELLs do not show what NCLB calls adequate yearly progress (AYP) in that particular content area, adaptations to instruction can be implemented to address the ELLs' needs.

Second, classroom-based content area assessment can be used for reclassification. For example, the results that are collected could be used to determine whether ELLs are ready for the mainstream classroom or should stay in the English language support program. When decisions about reclassification are made, the ELLs should be assessed in both their English language development and their content area knowledge.

Finally, the third purpose of content area assessment is accountability. Indeed, there are many state and federal large-scale content area assessments that ELLs have to take. One might therefore propose to do away with classroom-based assessments. However, content area teachers are required to provide quality standards-based instruction in their classes, and they can do so only if they constantly assess their ELL students to see whether their instruction is successful.

One issue that is extremely critical for content area teachers is the English proficiency of their ELLs. In most cases, content area teachers are not language teachers. Because of state requirements and mandates, some of them have participated in workshops and training programs that are geared toward making content comprehensible for ELLs. However, many content area teachers still face an insurmountable task when they have ELLs in their classroom, simply because they think that the ELLs need to learn English first. Many content area teachers believe that ELLs must achieve full language proficiency before they can be transitioned to mainstream classrooms. However, this approach is not feasible in the current educational context. As we know, current educational legislation, more specifically NCLB, holds schools accountable for the academic achievement of all students, ELLs included. As a result, states require ELLs to be assessed in the content areas *while* they are learning English, not *after* they have reached full proficiency in English.

The Interface of Language and Content in Content Area Assessment: The Example of Mathematics

With the advent of NCLB, language and content are no longer treated as two separate domains that have to be taught and assessed independently. Content area teachers who have ELLs in their classes need to be aware that academic language development should be actively promoted as part of instruction. We often hear that mathematics is the universal language, and 2 plus 2 is always 4. However, even though the principles of math are universal, the way that math is taught and assessed varies quite considerably from country to country.

For example, in many countries, subtraction is tested by using simple math equations, such as $11 - 5 = \_\_$. However, in the United States, math assessments, especially large-scale tests, rely extensively on word problems. A word problem is a short passage with a question that requires working with numbers that are provided directly or, as is more often the case, indirectly. Here is an example of a typical word problem for elementary grade students (www3.telus.net/public/m.games/WEB/GNSSM/nssm.1.html):

A 7-year-old child picks up 5 shiny pebbles on the way to school. On the way home he picks up some more. At home he shows his mother that he has 11 pebbles. How many did he pick up on the way home?

A closer analysis reveals several ELL-related issues with this seemingly easy word problem. First, in order to be able to solve the problem, ELLs must be able to read all the words in the passage. According to Peregoy and Boyle (2008), a student needs to be able to read in English with roughly 98% word-recognition accuracy and with about 90% comprehension to be at the Independent Reading Level, which requires little, if any, help from teachers. The global, overall meaning of the story is essential to solving the math problem, so unknown words will prevent ELLs from putting the ideas together to form a story line. For example, the key word in the problem is *pebbles*. Some ELLs might be able to move further if the word is unknown to them, but most will lack the confidence to do so if they have doubts about the meaning. Anything below 90% in word recognition and below 70% in comprehension will put ELLs at the Frustration Reading Level, a level too difficult for ELLs, even with help from teachers.

Second, going back to the word problem example, the question may be confusing for ELLs because *pebbles* is not in it. Most native English speakers will not notice the fact that *pebbles* is absent from the question, but some ELLs might find this very puzzling. Another confusing aspect is the presence of the number 7. Some ELLs want to work directly with the numbers, and they might think that the problem can be solved by adding all the numbers in the story: $7 + 5 + 11$. The way that the passage is structured does not directly indicate that the word problem actually focuses on subtraction, and this will make it very difficult for ELLs, because they have to turn an additive situation into a subtractive one.

Word problems are frequent in math assessments. An analysis of the Florida Comprehensive Assessment Test (FCAT), a statewide assessment that is administered to students in Grades 3–12, reveals the importance of word problems in math tests and, implicitly, the importance of English language proficiency in the assessment of this particular content area. Coombe, Folse, and Hubley (2007) looked at the FCAT Math Test for Grade 4 that was given in 2005 and found that out of 40 questions, not one was expressed in the form of a simple math question, such as $2 + 2 = ?$. The questions consisted of 65% word problems accompanied by a map, a geometric figure, or a table of data and 35% word problems without any visual support.

Given the overwhelming importance of word problems in summative statewide standardized exams, math teachers must integrate word problems into their classroom-based assessments. One pedagogical suggestion is that they should teach (and use in their own assessment instruments) the language that is essential to answering word problems. The words can be compiled through an analysis of math texts, and they should be explicitly used in instruction and assessment. To be effective instructors in their content area, math teachers must realize the importance of language proficiency as a vehicle for conveying and understanding math knowledge, and they should be very active in developing it.

All content area teachers should strive to be not only effective instructors in their specialized discipline but also facilitators of language development for their ELLs, especially with academic language. Thus, this chapter will discuss key concepts about language in order to familiarize content area instructors with them, in light of the fact that most content area teachers are not linguists and might have limited knowledge on second language acquisition theories and principles.

The following sections of this chapter will introduce several pedagogically relevant notions about academic language in general and ELL-related issues with the language of math, science, and social studies assessments in particular. A model for an ELL-oriented assessment in the content areas will be proposed so that content area teachers will no longer feel intimidated by the task of creating measurements of academic progress for their nonnative English speakers.

Academic Language: Definition and Framework

Before creating an assessment instrument for their ELL students, content area teachers need to understand a fundamental distinction between language that is used in everyday conversation and language that is used in an academic setting. In many cases, ELLs who are able to carry on fluent social conversations, characterized by excellent grammar and a native-like accent, are performing very poorly in the classroom. Teachers have often attributed this disconnect between social and academic performance to learning disabilities, simply because they could not perceive the fundamental differences between the two types of language proficiency (Artiles & Ortiz, 2002). The research conducted in this area by Cummins (1994) has produced two critical constructs that might help non-linguists, such as content area teachers, to avoid a feeling of frustration when working with ELLs.

The first construct that Cummins (1994) proposed is termed *basic interpersonal communication skill,* or BICS. This is the language required for face-to-face communication, in which interactions rely heavily on context clues. ELLs acquire BICS very quickly. It is not unusual for an ELL to learn and understand basic words and phrases in a matter of days, and fluency in BICS can usually be reached in 1–3 years. ELLs learn BICS from their classmates, television, and day-to-day interactions.

Nevertheless, the language skills that are required in content area classrooms are different from the BICS proficiency that ELLs acquire relatively fast. Cummins (1994) proposed a second construct of language proficiency that is applicable to classroom-based language interactions. This context-specific type of proficiency is called *cognitive-academic language proficiency,* or CALP. CALP usually takes more time to acquire, and an ELL might need anywhere from 5 to 10 years to catch up academically in English.

CALP, the language of school, is more complex and more demanding than BICS, or everyday language. A comparison of social and academic language activities might be helpful for content area teachers in order to understand which activities pose the highest degree of complexity for their ELLs.

First, there is social language in which there are a lot of context clues. This is called *context-embedded social language–BICS* and is exemplified by language used by ELLs on the playground, when ordering food in the cafeteria, and when interacting with native speakers outside the classroom in social settings where there is an abundance of nonverbal clues (e.g., facial expressions and gestures).

However, social language does not always occur in a setting where the context facilitates language communication and comprehension. There is also *context-reduced social language–BICS*, which is used by ELLs when they are conducting telephone conversations or filling out job applications with no model to follow.

CALP also has two identifiable categories of language that are separated by the degree to which the context is present in the setting. There is *context-embedded CALP*, which is employed by ELLs when they write book reports using a template, present an academic paper, or do math with manipulatives. There is also *context-reduced CALP*, which is employed by ELLs when they take standardized tests, listen to lectures, or do math word problems.

It is vital for content area teachers to remember that full proficiency in social language is not any indication of full proficiency in academic language. The fact that ELLs can point to the correct answer does not mean that they will provide the correct answer to science-test items without visuals. We frequently hear teachers say, "I don't know why this child can't read in my class. I just had a wonderful conversation with him about his weekend, and he speaks perfect English. I guess we have to refer him to special ed." If teachers understood the difference between the two types of language proficiency, they would be less likely to refer ELLs to special education programs when all these students really need is help with the development of their academic language.

Against this argument, some teachers might think that, if ELLs are failing in general education, perhaps they will receive more individualized instruction in special education classes. However, research shows that ELLs that have been placed in special education because of reported learning disabilities demonstrate lower verbal and full-scale IQ scores after placement in special education than at their initial evaluations. This indicates that even in special education, ELLs do not receive the type of instruction they need because some special education professionals lack instructional methodology and other professional development needed to serve the ELL population (Artiles & Ortiz, 2002).

The Language of Content Area Tests (and Texts)

A vital component of academic language proficiency, the language that is used in content area materials and assessments can pose many comprehension problems for ELLs. To understand why ELLs have difficulty with the acquisition of academic language, it will be useful to briefly look at the features of vocabulary, grammar, and syntax that are specific to content areas.

Vocabulary

Knowledge of vocabulary is essential for ELLs who want to communicate in academic settings successfully. Scarcella (2003) identified three types of words that are characteristic of academic language: general, technical, and academic. General words, such as *often* and *empty*, are non-specialized and are used in all content areas. Technical words are specialized and are used in specific fields. Examples of technical words are *divisor, coefficient*, and *quotient* in math; *atom* and *electron* in science; and *feudalism* and *republic* in social studies. Finally, academic words are both specialized and non-specialized and can be used in different content areas. These words pose a great deal of difficulty for ELLs. For example, an ELL might know the everyday meaning of *table* but might be confused when the word is used in math or science.

It is very easy to see how ELLs who have a good grasp of social English might have problems comprehending science materials or assessments when academic language is involved. An example of vocabulary confusion was provided by a content area teacher who was surprised to see an ELL in her class draw a picture in the response box during a test. Reading the prompt, the teacher noted that the item required test takers to "draw a conclusion." The ELL had taken the social meaning of the word into account and had started drawing the answer to the question. However, in content area tests assessments and instructional material, *draw* mostly occurs in combination with *conclusion* and therefore has nothing to do with the physical act of drawing.

An additional complexity of academic language is represented by the many ways in which the same academic concept can be conveyed during instruction and implicitly present in assessments. In mathematics, effective control of this type of vocabulary becomes crucial for ELLs in solving word problems. For example, ELLs have to know that the operation of addition can be signaled by any of these six terms: *add, and, plus, combine, sum*, and *increased by*. Prepositions can be very problematic for ELLs in math classes, too; an example is *divided by* versus *divided into* (Crandall, 1985).

In addition to the comprehension problems posed by isolated vocabulary words, the technical vocabulary of a content area includes complex combinations of words and phrases. There are simple fixed expressions, exemplified by *such as*, *for example*, and *for instance*, and more complex ones, like *greatest common factor* and *least common multiple*. The latter phrase is an example of a problematic math term that ELLs might have difficulty comprehending. It is very hard for ELLs to gather the specialized math meaning of the phrase if they attempt to process it in a word-by-word fashion using a dictionary, as they would normally do with an isolated word. In this case, the instruction should treat the phrase as an indivisible chunk so that when ELLs see it in an assessment, they do not attempt to separate it into components and translate each word. Appendix B contains a list of academic words content area teachers should concentrate on during their instruction and assessment for the benefit of their ELLs.

Grammar and Syntax

The academic language in content area assessment includes the typical grammar competence of social English, such as the tense system of English verbs, as well as additional grammatical and syntactic structures that are not frequently used in everyday social language. Among these structures are subject-verb agreement for irregular nouns, conditional sentences, passive voice, and relative phrases and clauses.

Based on their experiences with everyday conversations, ELLs might acquire the basic subject-verb agreement in English. The vast majority of nouns in social English are regular—that is, they add an *s* to the end to make the plural form. Thus, most ELLs know that they have to change the verb in the sentence "My book is on the desk" if they use the plural noun *books*: "My books *are* on the desk." In academic English, however, many nouns do not add an *s* to the end to form the plural, such as *criterion*, *crisis*, and *bacillus*, whose plurals are, respectively, *criteria*, *crises*, and *bacilli*. For that reason, subject-verb agreement, which is a very fundamental component of grammar proficiency, can become problematic for ELLs when they have to use irregular nouns.

Conditional sentences represent another problematic aspect of academic English. Some ELLs might have a hard time solving the following math problem, which is stated using *if* as a signal for a hypothetical situation: "If Tommy can run a lap in 2 minutes, how much time does he need to run 3 laps?" Nevertheless, the same student might be able to solve the problem if it was stated without *if*: "Tommy can run a lap in 2 minutes. How much time does he need to run 3 laps?"

In terms of English syntax, the passive voice (e.g., "When 20 *is divided* by 4" or "When 2 *is added* to a number"), and mathematics, one of the main difficulties for ELLs is the absence of a one-to-one correspondence between the math symbols and the words they represent. For example, take the following statement: "The number *a* is five less than the number *b*." If this were translated word for word by ELL students, it might be recorded as "a = 5 – b" rather than the correct translation, "a = b – 5." Research in this area has shown that ELLs have the tendency to apply to math text the same rules of grammar and syntax that they employ when they read and write standard, non-math text (Corasaniti Dale & Cuevas, 1992).

Complex sentences are another characteristic of content area assessments that can affect comprehension for ELLs. We have emphasized the linear approach that ELLs use when they process reading materials in English. Such an approach is not very productive with complex sentences that include multiple clauses. An examination of assessment items reveals that a large number of them are represented by very complex sentences. In science, we might have the following example: "We have learned that a plant is one type of living thing and an animal is another type. Can you give examples of living things belonging to these two types?" In social studies, we often find items similar to:

> In the Gettysburg Address, President Lincoln said that Union soldiers had sacrificed their lives to ensure that "government of the people, by the people, for the people shall not perish from the earth." What type of government was Lincoln referring to?

There are roughly three clauses that constitute the sentence: (a) In the Gettysburg Address, President Lincoln said (b) that Union soldiers had sacrificed their lives to ensure that (c)"government of the people, by the people, for the people shall not perish from the earth." Moreover, the sentence has four verbs (*said, had sacrificed, to ensure,* and *shall not perish*), three in very complex tenses (*said*: past tense simple; *had sacrificed*: past perfect simple; *shall not perish*: modal) and one in the infinitive (*to ensure*). Because of this type of language complexity, it is easy to understand the confusion that is experienced by ELLs who are reading this type of test item, especially if they try to process it word by word. They will probably be perplexed by the intricacy of the sentence and will be unable to look at the sentence globally to construct its meaning.

Clearly, for ELLs, the complex academic language that is used in content areas is often difficult to grasp. However, if content area teachers understand that they have to emphasize both content and language in their instruction and assessment, the ELLs in their classes will perform very well in summative large-scale standardized assessments and show they are within the acceptable parameters of AYP, as mandated by NCLB. The next section will provide teachers with an assessment design model that accounts for the language and academic needs of ELLs.

A Model for Designing and Implementing Classroom-Based Content Area Assessments for English Language Learners

We have noted how important language proficiency is in gathering valid data on ELLs' actual level of competency in the content areas. Classroom teachers and designers of large-scale tests should always consider the following questions: Is my test a true measure of content area knowledge, or is it more a measure of language proficiency? Will students with limited proficiency in English be able to demonstrate academic progress when they take this content area assessment?

To answer these questions, a model of designing and implementing classroom-based assessments in the content areas that takes into account the unique language needs of ELLs is proposed. For this student population, the assessment of content area proficiency can and should occur at all stages of academic language development.

The proposed model, shown in Figure 11, has several recommendations for content area educators. These recommendations are divided into three major categories: those that apply to the design stage of classroom assessment, those that should be implemented during test administration, and those that should be applied at the grading and/or feedback dissemination phases.

Figure 11.   A Model for Assessing ELLs in the Content Areas

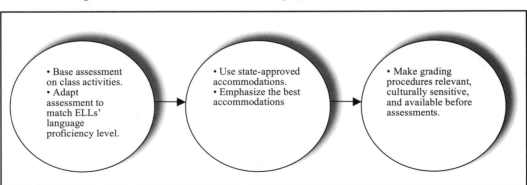

At the design stage, content area teachers should first look at their classroom activities and assess if they reflect curricular objectives in a clear and direct manner. It is very important that content area instructors base their content area measurements of knowledge on these activities. In addition, to design effective and valid assessments, content area teachers should be very familiar with the basics of academic language proficiency, especially with the various stages that ELLs go through in their language development.

At the administration stage, content area teachers should look at the test accommodations that are available in their state for large-scale standardized tests. They should make sure that their ELL students become familiar with these approved state accommodations in a classroom-based testing environment before they have to take large-scale assessments. Many state accommodation policies for ELLs stipulate that the accommodations are allowed if they have been used in the classroom, if the ELLs are familiar with them, and if they are requested by the ELLs or their parents.

At the grading or feedback stage, it is very important to make the grading procedures available beforehand and to provide relevant feedback to ELLs. Feedback that is relevant to ELLs should take into account the cultural differences that might exist between the values of ELLs and the values of mainstream America. In other words, a grade on a test is not sufficient; an explanation that is useful and culturally sensitive should always accompany it.

The Design Phase

Base the Assessment on Class Activities

Classroom instruction and assessment should always be based on clearly stated academic objectives. A well-defined list of academic objectives is extremely helpful for assessment purposes so that the teachers can make sure that important content is measured through their classroom-based instruments. Figure 12 provides a set of guiding questions that are linked to instruction and assessment.

It is pedagogically beneficial that the instruments for classroom assessment are based on classroom activities, which in turn are based on the curricular standards. We have previously noted that all the states have some form of large-scale content area tests that reflect statewide curricular standards. The suggestion here is not to teach to the standardized test, but simply to make sure that classroom instruction and subsequent activities cover the academic content that will be tested on the state test. In doing so, content area teachers will enable their ELLs to achieve test scores that will be a true measure of their abilities in any content area.

Figure 12.   Guidelines for Linking Instruction to Assessment

Guiding Question   **Instruction or Assessment Progression**

Guiding Question		Instruction or Assessment Progression

Am I proficient in the curricular standards in the teaching sequence?

Yes   No

Curricular Standards for the Content Areas

Are my classroom objectives based on curricular standards?

Yes   No

Classroom Objectives

Are my classroom activities based on classroom objectives?

Yes   No

Classroom Activities

Are my classroom assessments based on classroom activities?

Yes   No

Classroom Assessments

Are there are any gaps in the achievement of my classroom objectives?

Yes   No

Reteach or Reassess Identified Gaps

Repeat process with the next set of standards in the sequence.

One of the social studies standards for Grade 6 in California is WH6.4.4: *Explain the significance of Greek mythology to the everyday life of people in the region and how Greek literature continues to permeate our literature and language today, drawing from Greek mythology and epics, such as Homer's* Iliad *and* Odyssey *and from Aesop's* Fables.

Based on this standard, a social science teacher may define the following class objective: "Students will be able to identify the influence of Greek myths on the English language." A possible class activity is shown in Figure 13.

A format similar to this class activity should be used for the assessment of the class objective in focus. If the assessment shows that ELLs have mastered this class objective, they will probably have no problem with a multiple choice item that tests the same curricular standard, like the one shown in Figure 14.

The link between classroom activities and classroom assessments is very important for ELLs. When content area teachers administer classroom-based assessments, they should make sure that the format is a familiar one for ELLs. In addition, all tasks should mirror the activities that have already been used

Figure 13.   Sample Activity for Class Objective

Look at the following words:

atlas

herculean

olympian

1. Without using the dictionary, write a definition for each word listed above.

atlas _____

herculean _____

olympian _____

2. All these words can be traced back to a person or a place in Greek mythology. What is the name or place for each of them?

atlas _____

herculean _____

olympian _____

Figure 14.   Multiple Choice Item for Class Objective

atlas — a collection of maps
herculean — very powerful
labyrinth — a maze
olympian — majestic, honored

All these words in the English language today originated in the myths of the

A. Romans

B. Chinese

C. Greeks

D. Egyptians

---

during instruction—not just once, but repeatedly. Because the format is familiar and has already been practiced by ELLs, the assessment will measure content and not test anxiety.

Adapt the Assessment to Match ELLs' Level of Language Proficiency

A clearly established link between instruction and assessment is a necessary but not sufficient condition for a reliable and valid measure of content area knowledge for ELLs. Content area instructors must go further and make sure that their assessments also take into account ELLs' language proficiency.

Understanding the importance of the link between language and academic content, the Teachers of English to Speakers of Other Languages (TESOL) organization designed a new set of language proficiency standards for ELLs in pre-K–12 in the United States in 2006. These new standards are:

- Standard 1 (S1): ELLs communicate for social, intercultural, and instructional purposes within the school setting.

- Standards 2–5: ELLs communicate the information, ideas, and concepts that are necessary for academic success in the area of language arts (S2), mathematics (S3), science (S4), and social studies (S5).

These standards recognize that content area instruction is an integral part of language development, and they are a response to the provisions of the

NCLB, which requires the states to develop language proficiency standards that are grounded in state academic content standards (TESOL, 2006).

How can these standards help content area teachers to create more effective assessment tools? To answer this question, we will organize a matrix that contains five levels of language proficiency, four language domains, grade-level clusters, content topics, and samples of performance indicators.

In the TESOL (2006) standards, there are five levels of language proficiency, as shown in Figure 15.

The new TESOL levels of language proficiency follow a tradition in the field of second language acquisition that has started with Krashen's theory of second language acquisition. Therefore, it is beneficial to briefly examine the basic principles of Krashen's view regarding the acquisition of another language. His theory encompasses five hypotheses (Krashen, 1985):

- Acquisition versus Learning: fluency is due to what has been acquired in an environment that replicates the natural way in which humans acquire their first language. Language cannot be learned because too much 'learning' bogs one down in rules and forms.

- Monitor Hypothesis: a direct result of learning, the monitor is an internal set of explicit grammar rules learners employ when they have time to think about the accuracy of their utterances, e.g., when they write in a second language. According to Krashen, the monitor hinders acquisition in early stages and ought to be avoided.

Figure 15.   The Five Levels of English Proficiency

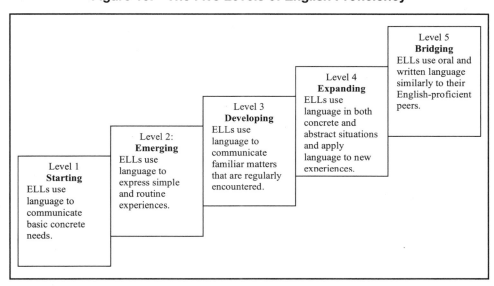

- Natural Order: we acquire language in a predictable or natural order

- Input (i+1): According to Krashen, comprehensible input is the only true source of second language acquisition. A condition for language acquisition is that the person acquiring the language understand input language that contains structure a bit beyond his or her current level of competence (hence i +1). In other words, we should expose ELLs to language that is just above their level. They should be able to understand most of it but still be challenged because they won't understand all of it.

- Affective Filter: best acquisition will occur in environments where anxiety level is low. If the affective filter is up, language acquisition is hindered. If the affective filter is down, language acquisition is promoted.

Stages of Second Language Development

Based on Krashen's theory of second language acquisition, Krashen and Terrell developed a teaching approach called the Natural Approach. Part of this approach was a model for second language acquisition, which contained four stages, as described below:

I.   **Preproduction**: At this stage, which may last anywhere from 10 hours to six months, ELLs might have a vocabulary of up to 500 words they can understand, but may not be confident enough to use them. This stage often involves a 'silent period': ELLs may not speak, but can respond by pointing, performing, gesturing, nodding, or responding with a simple "yes" or "no."

II. **Early Production**: This stage may last an additional six months after preproduction. ELLs' vocabulary may contain approximately 1,000 words they are able to understand and use. ELLs can usually speak in one- or two-word phrases, and can respond to comprehension questions by giving short answers to simple questions, e.g., yes/no, or who/what/where.

III. **Speech Emergence**: This stage may last up to another year after early production. ELLs at this stage can use short phrases and simple sentences to communicate and have around 3,000 words in their vocabulary. They are able to ask simple questions, and can answer simple questions. When they produce longer sentences, their language contains grammatical errors that can interfere with meaning.

IV. **Intermediate Fluency**: This stage may last another year after speech emergence. ELLs' vocabulary might be close to 6,000 words. Additionally, they are able to make complex statements, state their opinions, ask for clarifications when necessary, and speak at greater length.

Stage	Characteristics	Time Frame	Teacher Prompts
Preproduction	Has minimal comprehension: does not verbalize; nods "Yes" and "No" ; draws and points	0–6 months	Show me... Circle the... Where is...? Who has...?
Early Production	Has limited comprehension: produces one- or two-word responses; participates using key words and familiar phrases; uses present-tense verbs	6 months–1 year	Yes/no questions; Either/or questions; One- or two-word answers; Lists; Labels
Speech Emergence	Has good comprehension: can produce simple sentences; makes grammar and pronunciation errors; frequently misunderstands jokes	1–3 years	Why...? How...? Explain... Phrase or short -sentence answers
Intermediate Fluency	Has excellent comprehension: makes few grammatical errors	3–5 years	What would happen if...? Why do you think...?

California's English Language Proficiency Levels

The model of language acquisition developed by Krashen and Terrell has been used by many states when they developed their own proficiency levels of second language acquisition. For example, California has a test for assessing language development for their ELLs called the California English Language Development Test (CELDT). The test covers four skill areas (listening, speaking, reading, and writing) and contains five proficiency levels (beginning, early intermediate, intermediate, early advanced, and advanced). Teachers in all areas could use the CELDT proficiency descriptors to match language development objectives with the linguistic needs of their ELLs. The table below provides a description of the five levels of the CELDT, adapted from Diaz-Rico (2008):

Level	Listening/Speaking	Reading	Writing
Beginning	May be able to recognize and speak a few isolated words	May be able to recognize a few isolated words	May be able to write a few isolated words.
Early Intermediate	Can produce words or phrases. Can separate spoken sounds into words. Can respond to questions using simple vocabulary	Can recognize words and phrases in print. Can match words to pictures	Can write a simple sentence following a writing prompt
Intermediate	Can produce relevant sentences using progressively more complex vocabulary	Can read text with basic comprehension	Can write several sentences following a writing prompt. Can write a story with a sequence of events
Early Advanced	Can understand and respond to instructional delivery	Can comprehend text using inferencing, drawing conclusions, and making predictions	Can write well-organized and well-formed sentences and paragraphs
Advanced	Can understand and respond to complex instructional delivery	Can comprehend narrative and expository texts requiring a range of thinking skills	Can write paragraphs and essays with effective organization, few grammatical errors, and specific vocabulary

Language Development and Cultural Adaptation

Recognizing the importance of culture in the process of language acquisition, Ernst-Slavit, Moore, and Maloney (2002) looked at the language proficiency stages from the language and culture perspective, adding suggestions for teachers and instructional activities to be used with ELLs at various stages of language development, as seen in the table below:

Stage	Linguistic Considerations	Cultural Considerations	Suggestions for Teachers	Effective Activities
Preproduction	• Communicates with gestures, actions, and verbal formulas • Is building receptive vocabulary • Is recycling learning language practice • Benefits from listening/compre-hension activities	• Silent period: Teachers should not force ELLs to speak until they are ready to do so.	• Create a stress-free environment • Provide support and encouragement • Avoid asking direct questions	• Face-to-face conversation • Simple demonstrated directions • Participation in art/music/PE • Puzzles/games, real objects, or manipulatives • Picture books • Encouraging drawing
Early Production	• Intuitively under-stands that English is a system • Labels and categorizes • Encounters native language inter-ference • Uses one- and two-word responses and chunks of language • Can say, "I don't understand."	• Cultural fatigue: gradual accumulation, day by day, of stress derived from the many differences in the new culture	• Monitor error correction • Use list of key terms for previewing • Use audiotapes of readings and lectures • Use graphic organizers	• Low-level questions • Picture books with simple texts • Simple written responses • Copying words and sentences • Oral reading
Speech Emergence	• Uses language purposefully • Produces complete sentences	• Tension between assimilation and acculturation • Recovering from previous frustration and fatigue	• Use frequent comprehension checks • Design lessons focusing on concepts • Introduce expanded vocabulary	• Demonstration • Simple oral presentations • Answering higher-level questions • Hands-on activities • Small group work
Intermediate Fluency	• Can produce connected narrative • Can use reading and writing incorporated into lesson • Can write answers to higher level questions • Can resolve conflicts verbally	• Cultural adjustment: ELLs feel at home in the new culture, and have successfully adjusted to the norms and standards of the new environment	• Validate students' languages and cultures	• Content explanations • Paragraph writing • Reading for infor-mation in content areas • Summaries, outlines, reports • Explanations of new ideas/concepts • Workbooks, work-sheets, and tests

Beyond Krashen: The New PreK–K TESOL Standards and Language Proficiency Levels

With the advent of No Child Left Behind legislation, the proficiency standards for ELLS had to adapt to the new focus of directly and explicitly linking English language development with academic knowledge expansion. Consequently, the TESOL organization developed new standards with a focus on core content areas, as discussed in Chapter 4. Additionally, new language proficiency levels have been introduced with a focus on content areas, as seen in Appendix A.

In the new standards, there are five levels of language proficiency.

Level 1, Starting. At this level of proficiency, ELLs have little or no understanding of English, and most of the time they respond nonverbally to simple commands or questions. ELLs build meaning from text from nonprint elements such as illustrations, graphs, and tables. Therefore, content area teachers should select texts that are rich in illustrations, or, if such texts are not available, they should make illustrations, graphs, or charts available to ELLs as supplementary materials.

Level 2, Emerging. At this level of proficiency, ELLs are beginning to understand phrases and short sentences. They can convey limited information in routine situations by using memorized chunks of language. These ELLs are beginning to use general academic vocabulary and familiar expressions in everyday communication.

Level 3, Developing. At this level of proficiency, ELLs have a more developed vocabulary and are starting to understand more complex speech. They speak English spontaneously, using simple sentences that are both comprehensible and appropriate but that are frequently marked by grammatical errors. These ELLs understand specific as well as general academic vocabulary. They still have some problems understanding and producing complex structures and academic language.

Level 4, Expanding. At this level of proficiency, ELLs have language skills that are adequate for everyday communication demands, but they still make occasional structural and lexical errors. They are proficient in communicating in new and unfamiliar settings, but they have some difficulty with complex language structures and abstract academic concepts.

Level 5, **Bridging**. Even though these ELLs are not yet fully proficient in English, they can express themselves fluently and accurately on a wide range of social and academic topics in a variety of contexts. They need very minimal language support to function in English-based instructional environments.

In the TESOL (2006) proficiency standards, there are four language domains—listening, speaking, reading, and writing—and five grade-level clusters: pre-K–K, 1–3, 4–5, 6–8, and 9–12.

The content topics that we are going to use have been selected from national and state academic content standards. For example, for the social studies pre-K–K standards, the academic content area selection contains the themes of community workers, families, transportation, clothing, food, shelter, classroom, school, neighborhood, friends, holidays, and symbols.

The performance indicators are examples of measurable language behavior that ELLs are expected to demonstrate as they engage in classroom activities. Sample performance indicators consist of three elements: content, language function, and support or strategy. Here is an example of a performance indicator for math: "State or repeat [language function] the steps in problem solving [content] using manipulatives or visual support [support]."

The matrix that we have constructed in Table 15 shows how these standards are operationalized, using the five levels of language proficiency, the four language domains, the grade-level clusters, the content topics, and the samples of performance indicators.

Because of the direct link between academic content knowledge and language proficiency, content area instructors should make use of these standards when they create assessments for their ELLs in their classrooms. A critical step in using these content area–focused language proficiency standards is the identification of ELLs' language proficiency level. To do this, content area teachers may rely on their own assessment of ELLs' language proficiency by utilizing the descriptors for language proficiency discussed earlier. They may also use the information that is collected through language proficiency tests that states are now mandated to develop and administer due to NCLB.

Once the level of language proficiency is identified for ELLs, content area teachers can easily develop assessment instruments based on the TESOL standards. For example, let us suppose that a third grade science teacher has an ELL who is at the second level of language proficiency, emerging. The science teacher wants to design a written assessment for that student and consults the TESOL language proficiency standards, in this case Standard 4. The performance indicators for writing at that level for that standard state: "Draw and describe physical attributes of local plant and animal species from real-life observations, experience, or pictures." Figure 16 shows an assessment tool based on this performance indicator.

Table 15.   TESOL Standards Matrix

Topics (S1) Grades Pre-K–K	Classroom	Family	Rules and games	Social behavior
Language Domains	Reading	Writing	Listening	Speaking
Level 1, Starting	Match words with pictures on word walls or bulletin boards.	Draw family members.	Identify objects from pictures or realia as directed orally.	Practice simple polite expressions, such as *please* and *thank you*.
Level 2, Emerging	Identify letters in the names of classroom objects in pictures or text.	Label photos or drawing of family members or friends using letters or scribble writing.	Follow one-step oral directions in groups in games and activities.	Make polite requests of teachers or classmates.
Level 3, Developing	Match names of familiar objects with pictures or realia.	Write descriptions of family members using drawings, letters, scribble writing, or words with invented spelling.	Follow multiple-step oral directions with partners in activities and games.	Role-play conversations with adults using polite language.
Level 4, Expanding	Identify words and phrases that are school-related, such as *entrance* and *exit*.	Write stories of family experiences using drawings, letters, scribble writing, or words and phrases with invented spelling.	Demonstrate rules explained by the teacher in activities and games.	Offer apologies and give compliments in small group environments.
Level 5, Bridging	Build meaning from picture books with text.	Write notes to family members using words and phrases with invented spelling.	Respond to commands while engaged in activities and games.	Adapt language appropriate to familiar audiences.

Topics (S2) Grades 1–3	Story grammar	Homophones, compound words	Phonics, phonemic awareness	Rhyming words
Language Domains	Reading	Writing	Listening	Speaking
Level 1, Starting	Identify story elements such as characters and settings in illustrated stories.	Fill in vocabulary from illustrations with a partner.	Identify sounds nonverbally (by clapping or gestures) in small groups.	Practice saying illustrated minimal pairs (*pat-bat*) with a partner.
Level 2, Emerging	Categorize story elements in illustrated stories using graphic organizers by characters, setting, or events.	Match vocabulary to illustrated word charts, games, or other materials with a partner.	Make distinctions between regular and irregular words through gestures with a partner.	Repeat phrases associated to illustrations in large and small groups.
Level 3, Developing	Sequence story events in illustrated stories (beginning, middle, end).	Use vocabulary to design word walls, puzzles, or language patterns with a partner.	Identify affixes and root words through gestures with a partner.	Create sentences based on familiar word families or topics in small groups.
Level 4, Expanding	Match transition words (e.g., *so*, *after*) or phrases with sequence, main ideas, or details in illustrated stories.	Write visually supported text from vocabulary banks and resources with a partner.	Replicate through gestures, stress, and intonation patterns of rhymes, prose, or poetry with a partner.	Perform rhymes or verses developed with a partner.
Level 5, Bridging	Identify and order main ideas and details in language-modified grade-level stories.	Create original text from vocabulary resources.	Identify the musical elements of literary language through simulation.	Create and recite original verses or poetry.

Table 15.   TESOL Standards Matrix (continued)

Topics (S3) Grades 4–5	Three-dimensional shapes, polygons, angles	Data analysis	Patterns, relations, functions	Basic operations
Language Domains	Reading	Writing	Listening	Speaking
Level 1, Starting	Sort figures by characteristics from labeled visuals and objects (four sides, three angles)	Label variables from tables, charts, and graphs with a partner.	Recognize algebraic symbols or elements from oral commands with visual support.	State and confirm math operations represented visually.
Level 2, Emerging	Match characteristics and properties from visuals, objects, and phrases (e.g., *the left angle of the square*).	Formulate and answer questions from tables, charts, and graphs with a partner.	Match phrases to algebraic symbols or elements from visually supported spoken statements.	Relate how to solve problems from provided models with a partner.
Level 3, Developing	Distinguish among figures from text supported by illustrations.	Organize and describe information in tables, charts, and graphs with a partner.	Identify relationships between algebraic symbols or functions according to spoken descriptions with visual support.	Share steps outlined to solve everyday problems with a partner.
Level 4, Expanding	Construct or draw figures by following steps in visually supported text.	Write paragraphs using information in tables, charts, and graphs.	Sort algebraic math sentences according to spoken descriptions with graphic support.	Give everyday examples of how to solve problems with a partner or in small groups.
Level 5, Bridging	Infer geometric relationships among figures from language-modified grade-level text.	Summarize and apply information in tables, charts, and graphs to new situations.	Analyze change and identify transformation in various contexts from spoken descriptions.	Apply information from solving problems to everyday situations.

Topics (S4) Grades 6–8	Body systems, organs	Weather, climate zones, natural disasters	Atoms, cells, molecules	Solar system
Language Domains	Reading	Writing	Listening	Speaking
Level 1, Starting	Match words or phrases to diagrams or models.	Draw and label charts of features, conditions, or occurrences, using newspapers or online resources.	Identify elements within models or diagrams, following oral directions.	Repeat definitions of key objects in the solar system with a partner.
Level 2, Emerging	Classify short descriptions of body systems using visual support.	Describe features, conditions, and occurrences around the world based on newspapers or online resources.	Match oral descriptions of functions of various elements with models or diagrams.	Describe the appearance and composition of objects in the solar system with a partner,.
Level 3, Developing	Find or sort visually supported information about processes (e.g., white cells versus red cells).	Compare features, conditions, and occurrences between two geographical areas based on information from multiple sources.	Arrange models or diagrams based on sequential oral directions.	Compare appearance and composition of objects in a galaxy with a partner.
Level 4, Expanding	Create sequenced steps to illustrate processes based on visually supported text.	Write a personal account describing the impact of features, conditions, or occurrences around the world, using multiple sources.	Reproduce models and diagrams based on visually supported materials.	Discuss or present illustrated processes involving planetary objects.
Level 5, Bridging	Make predictions from language-modified grade-level materials.	Interpret global impact of various features, conditions, or occurrences from language-modified grade-level material.	Design models or diagrams from texts without visual support.	Explain in technical vocabulary the structure of the universe using examples of planetary components.

Table 15.   TESOL Standards Matrix (*continued*)

Topics (S5) Grades 9–12	Global economy, supply and demand, money and banking	Cultural diversity and cohesion, international and multinational organizations	Supreme Court cases; federal, civil, and individual rights; social issues and inequities	Human populations
Language Domains	Reading	Writing	Listening	Speaking
Level 1, Starting	Connect areas on maps or globes and their products or monetary units, using visually supported sources.	Brainstorm in small groups and record examples of multicultural institutions or symbols.	Find basic information in illustrations and photographs after listening to oral statements,.	Exchange with a partner facts about peoples, languages, or cultures of local communities or native countries.
Level 2, Emerging	Gather information about places, products, or monetary units from newspapers, charts, or graphs.	List and define multicultural issues, symbols, or institutions in small groups.	Identify topics or political issues in illustrations and photographs after listening to oral descriptions.	Share personal experiences and reactions to migration or immigration with a partner.
Level 3, Developing	Identify trends in monetary values or production from charts, tables, or graphs.	Compare ideal and real situations for multicultural issues or organizations, using graphic organizers.	Compare oral summaries of political situations and visual representations.	Discuss demographic shifts, migration, immigration, languages, or cultures in small groups.
Level 4, Expanding	Predict future trends in monetary values or production from visually supported text.	State and defend a position on multicultural issues or organizations, using feedback from a partner.	Interpret peer reenactments or presentations based on political situations as seen in the media.	Explain the effect of demographic shifts or migration on peoples, languages, or cultures in small groups.
Level 5, Bridging	Interpret economic trends based on language-modified grade-level materials.	Write essays or poems that address or pose creative solutions to multicultural issues.	Evaluate mock trials or political speeches produced by classmates.	Present orally the characteristics, distribution, and migration of peoples, their languages, and their cultures.

Figure 16.   Assessment Tool Example

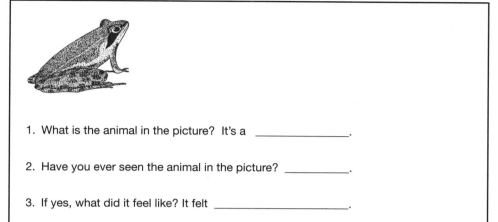

1. What is the animal in the picture? It's a _____.

2. Have you ever seen the animal in the picture? _____.

3. If yes, what did it feel like? It felt _____.

4. Write down everything you can think of about the animal in the picture.

One great characteristic of the TESOL language proficiency standards is that they are not rigid and can be transformed quite easily. In this example, the science teacher can easily make a change in the language domain of assessment, from writing to speaking. Instead of asking ELLs to write the answers to the questions, the science teacher can ask them to respond orally to the task. In other words, if content area teachers make these types of changes, they have a very comprehensive assessment-building tool at their disposal and may be confident that their assessment focuses on both language proficiency and content knowledge.

The Administration Phase

Use State-Approved Accommodations in the Classroom

Chapter 3 discussed the five most common types of accommodations for ELLs in large-scale assessments: additional time, the use of a dictionary, individual or small-group administration, flexible scheduling, and reading the test aloud in English. An accommodation is effective if it levels the playing field for ELLs by reducing the impact that English language proficiency might have on test performance. We also noted that research in the area of accommodation effectiveness is very limited and that many times the same accommodation renders contrasting results when it is used by different groups of ELLs. In spite of these limitations, before more conclusive research becomes available, content area teachers should try to use state-sanctioned accommodations in their classroom-based assessments especially on tests, so that the ELLs in their class become familiarized with them.

For content area teachers, the first step in putting these accommodations into practice is to become familiar with what accommodation policies their states have for content area tests. Chapter 3 contains a very detailed, state-by-state description of these policies at the state level. For one reason or another, these accommodations are often not known by K–12 teachers, content area or otherwise. If teachers do not know what is allowed and what is not, they cannot implement accommodations in their classroom assessments. When teachers do not employ test accommodations, ELLs become unaware that these accommodations exist. The consequences are twofold. First, accommodations are not requested by ELLs in large-scale assessments, which raises the question of test fairness. Second, even when accommodations are requested by ELLs, their effectiveness is reduced if they are not used routinely in the classroom assessments; this is clearly stated in many state policy documents.

Emphasize the Best Accommodations

Once state-authorized accommodations are identified, content area teachers should do two things: They should adapt ELL accommodations to the demands and characteristics of their classrooms, and they should emphasize the accommodations that best reduce the language barrier for their ELLs.

An example of large-scale accommodations being adapted to classroom conditions and demands is the combination of extended time and flexible scheduling. In many states, ELLs are given more time than non-ELLs to finish a section of a test. For example, in Florida, one condition for this accommodation is that ELLs finish that test portion in one school day. However, for content area teachers, this accommodation cannot be used without adapting it to the regular school schedule that instruction and assessment have to follow. One adaptation, therefore, is to give ELLs take-home tests; another is to make portions of the test available for ELLs to work on at home. In these ways, ELLs will become familiar with the accommodation, and using it will not disrupt the regular time allocation for instruction and assessment.

When selecting accommodations for classroom assessment, content area teachers should focus on those that contribute significantly to the reduction of the negative impact that language proficiency might have on ELL test scores. Chapter 3 showed that many states allow either a bilingual dictionary with no definitions or an English dictionary during large-scale content area assessments. However, it is very difficult to see the effectiveness of this type of accommodation. For example, consider the meaning of the word *tell*. If ELLs who are taking a science test have access to an English dictionary, Figure 17 shows what that they would find if they consulted the popular Merriam-Webster English dictionary (www.m-w.com/dictionary/tell).

It is easy to see how ELLs could be overwhelmed by the number of definitions they find in a dictionary, especially since all definitions are equal for them. In many science tests, the word *tell* is synonymous with *indicate* or *reveal*, and these are not at the top of the list in Figure 17. Research has suggested that the use of a glossary is better; it could be located at the bottom of the test page or in the margins of the test, or it could be a student-made one to be consulted during the test. A typical glossary entry for a fifth grade test item

Figure 17.   Merriam-Webster's Definition of *Tell*

Main Entry: ¹tell
Pronunciation: 'tel

Function: *verb*

Inflected Form(s): told /' told/; tell·ing

Etymology: Middle English, from Old English *tellan;* akin to Old High German *zellen*, to count, tell; Old English *talu*, tale

transitive verb

1 : COUNT, ENUMERATE <*tell* the stars, if thou be able to number them —Genesis 15:5 (Authorized Version) >

2 a : to relate in detail : NARRATE <*told* the whole story to us> b : to give utterance to : SAY <could never *tell* a lie>

3 a : to make known : DIVULGE, REVEAL <don't *tell* your password> b : to express in words <she never *told* her love —Shakespeare>

4 a : to give information to : INFORM <*tell* us about your job> b : to assure emphatically <they did not do it, I *tell* you>

5 : ORDER, DIRECT <*told* me to wait>

6 : to find out by observing : RECOGNIZE <you can *tell* it's a masterpiece> *intransitive verb*

1 : to give an account <an article *telling* of her experience>

2 : to act as an informer—often used with *on* <I'll get even with you if you ever *tell* on me —*Inside Detective*>

3 : to have a marked effect <the pressure was beginning to *tell* on him>

4 : to serve as evidence or indication

synonym see REVEAL

from a required science test in Virginia (www.virginiasol.com/test_grade5.htm) is shown in Figure 18.

When ELLs have this type of support available to them, they can focus more on content instead of trying to decipher what the item actually requires them to do. It seems to be a more effective way to measure content than simply handing ELLs a dictionary along with the test. Therefore, if content area teachers have a choice of which accommodations to emphasize, they should select the ones that directly contribute to the assessment of content, not of language proficiency.

The Grading or Feedback Phase

Make Grading Procedures Relevant, Culturally Sensitive and Available Before Assessments

All students, but especially students who are learning content at the same time that they are learning English, need to have a good grasp of the assessment process that their content area teachers employ. ELLs need to have a good knowledge of the assessment process because it helps them to identify the fundamental points of academic knowledge. When ELLs have access to study guides, previous assessment instruments, and grading procedures and tools, they have full control over the assessment process from the beginning to the end, thus reducing test anxiety and increasing test validity and reliability.

For many content area instructors, evaluation rubrics are a very effective way to measure student understanding of an academic topic or principle. An example of a relevant scoring rubric for ELLs in social studies classrooms is provided by O'Malley and Pierce (1996). In many social studies classrooms, ELLs are required to produce either a short paragraph or an essay based on social studies prompts or topics. However, because ELLs are still in the process

---

Figure 18.   A Typical Glossary Entry for Fifth Grade Test

Satellites are useful for every reason except:

a. They enable us to communicate with people on the other side of the world

b. They help us predict the weather

c. They keep track of air traffic

d. They tell us about the core of the earth   *tell = give information*

e. They give military strategists views of other countries

of mastering language while mastering social studies content, clear scoring criteria should be created by content area teachers for an accurate and valid evaluation of both academic progress and English language development.

Drawing from the work of Baker et al. (1992) and Herman, Aschbacher, and Winters (1992). O'Malley and Pierce (1996) have created a general scoring rubric for grading report writing in social studies. Their rubric contains five criteria: principles or concepts, argument, prior knowledge of facts and events, text detail, and misconceptions. The principles or concepts criterion refers to the number of principles or concepts that ELLs introduced in their writing, such as immigration, slavery, and political parties. The second criterion, argument, identifies whether the writing shows evidence of a clear position supported by reasons and examples. The third criterion, prior knowledge of facts and events, focuses on the number of facts and events mentioned by the ELLs that are not part of the text on which the writing is based. The fourth criterion, text detail, looks at the number of facts and events in the writing that *are* based on the text. The last criterion, misconceptions, looks at whether the writing contains misconceptions or factual errors.

However, a social studies rubric based on these five criteria evaluates only the mastery of academic knowledge by ELLs and does not explicitly measure the features of the language that have been used in the assessment. With the already identified emphasis on the relationship between language proficiency and content area achievement, a rubric for assessing social studies report writing should also contain a language assessment component, such as that shown in Figure 19. A rubric that provides a score for social studies content and a score for writing proficiency will be a very relevant instrument for ELLs who want to know the levels of their language and content abilities.

Culture is an important variable to consider when designing grading procedures for ELLs. Content area teachers should be aware that grading procedures and the communication of assessment results must be clear and relevant as well as culturally sensitive, due to the possible cultural differences between the teachers and the ELLs.

Research has shown that culturally and linguistically diverse students might have different expectations about the classroom environment. If these expectations are not met by the ELLs' teachers and peers, then learning, class participation, and attendance are very likely to be negatively affected (Croniger, 1991; Good, 1993). An example of the different expectations of American and non-American students is provided by Niehoff, Turnley, and Yen (2001). Their study, which focused on the classroom expectations of American and Taiwanese students, found that the Taiwanese students expected more in-class group assignments (graded work, usually done outside of class), whereas the American students displayed higher expectations for in-class group activities (conducted during class, generally a non-traditional learning tool).

Figure 19.   Grading Rubric for Report Writing in Social Studies

Score	Content Performance Evaluation	Description
4	Outstanding Task Completion	• Principles or Concepts: Examines the problem or issues from several positions. • Argument: Takes a well-defined position with appropriate supporting evidence. • Prior Knowledge: Uses specific prior historical knowledge to examine the issues. • Text Detail: Cites appropriate detail from text to support an argument. • Misconceptions: Makes no misconceptions or factual errors.
3	Advanced Task Completion	• Principles or Concepts: Has a clear understanding of the problem or issues and identifies more than one aspect of the problem or issues. • Argument: Takes a definite but general position. • Prior Knowledge: Uses general ideas from prior historical knowledge with fair accuracy. • Text Detail: Connects only major text facts to basic issues. • Misconceptions: Makes errors in some factual or interpretive information.
2	Basic Task Completion	• Principles or Concepts: Shows a general understanding of the problem or issues. • Argument: Takes a position that is not well defined, with only generalities and opinion for support. • Prior Knowledge: Uses limited prior historical knowledge. • Text Detail: Makes few connection between text facts and basic issues. • Misconceptions: Makes occasional errors in facts and interpretation.
1	Minimal Task Completion	• Principles or Concepts: Shows little understanding of the problem or issues. • Argument: Takes a position that is not clear and that contains general unrelated statements. • Prior Knowledge: Makes no use of prior historical knowledge. • Text Detail: Repeats one or two unrelated facts. • Misconceptions: Makes frequent errors in facts and interpretation.

Score	Language Performance Evaluation	Description
4	Outstanding Task Completion	• Effective topic and idea development. • Excellent organization. • Variety in the use of language. • Control of sentence structure, grammar and usage, and mechanics.
3	Advanced Task Completion	• Moderate topic and idea development and organization. • Adequate, relevant details. • Some variety in language. • Few errors (not affecting comprehension) relative to the length of the essay or the complexity of sentence structure, grammar and usage, and mechanics.
2	Basic Task Completion	• Limited topic or idea development, organization, and/or details. • Errors that interfere somewhat with comprehension. • Too many errors relative to the length of the essay or the complexity of sentence structure, grammar and usage, and mechanics.
1	Minimal Task Completion	• Very limited topic or idea development, organization, and/or details. • Errors that seriously interfere with communication. • Little control of sentence structure, grammar and usage, and mechanics.

Content Performance Score   _____

Language Performance Score   _____

Total Score   _____

Recommendations: _____

This finding suggests that not all students will be equally accepting of in-class group activities (which are conducted by the teacher). American students are exposed to this type of activity from their early years on, whereas such practices are not as prevalent in Taiwan's educational system. Consequently, a student from Taiwan might expect more group assignments (for the students to do on their own) instead of group activities (moderated by the teacher), and if the content area teacher is not aware of this expectation, a student's educational progress might be hindered.

Scarcella (1992) identifies several areas that are of extreme importance when providing feedback to ELLs. The first is criticism and praise—specifically, the need for content area teachers to identify the most appropriate ways to provide criticism and praise to ELLs from a specific cultural background. The second sensitive area is error correction. Do ELLs value error correction, disregard it, or find it insulting? Should content area teachers correct the error directly or use a more indirect method, such as recast, as shown in the following example:

ELL: Lincoln was assassinate in 1865.
Content area teacher: So, Lincoln was assassinated in 1865.

It is important to know that not all cultures value indirect correction. Ran (2001) discovered that Chinese parents in the United States were disappointed with their children's teachers because the U.S. teachers did not provide enough critical feedback and direct correction to their children.

The third area identified by Scarcella (1992) is wait time. This is the gap between the end of the teacher's question and the beginning of the student's answer. In American classrooms, the wait time is around one second, whereas in other cultures it can be three to four seconds. Cultures with a relatively long wait time value thoughtful consideration of a question before a response is articulated. ELLs with this type of cultural background might think that their teacher is not assigning equal value to their answer if the teacher does not allow them a culturally appropriate amount of time in which to think about the answer.

Other areas of potential cultural conflict to which Scarcella (1992) directs content area teachers' attention are student requests for clarification (i.e., how ELLs request clarification and how these clarifications are interpreted by the teachers), teacher comprehension checks (i.e., how the teacher uses questions to check content comprehension and how these questions are interpreted by ELLs), and tolerance for standing out publicly (i.e., how ELLs feel about being singled out in class).

Things to Consider

- The fact that ELLs can communicate in social situations (BICS) does not mean they are fully proficient in academic language (CALP).

- Content area teachers should be careful not to mistake ELLs' language development issues as a learning disability.

- When developing classroom-based assessments, content area teachers should make sure that assessment matches ELLs' language proficiency level, thus measuring content knowledge and not English language proficiency.

- The developed classroom-based content area assessments should clearly reflect classroom activities ELLs in which ELLs have participated.

- Classroom-based content area assessments should include state-approved accommodations so when ELLs take large-scale standardized tests, they can recognize these accommodations.

- Grading procedures for classroom-based content area assessments should be made available before assessments. In addition, content area teachers should make grading relevant and culturally sensitive.

Chapter 5

Alternative Assessment Approaches in Content Area Classrooms for English Language Learners

This chapter will look at alternative assessment approaches. It will start by comparing the characteristics of alternative and traditional assessments and will continue with the analysis of three of the most popular alternative assessment instruments: performance assessment, curriculum-based measurement, and portfolios.

Alternative Assessment: Definition and Examples

In general, an alternative assessment is any type of assessment that requires students to perform, create, or do something by using tasks that correspond to meaningful instructional activities. Traditional assessments are best represented by timed multiple choice items in large-scale standardized tests, which are designed to focus on one correct answer. In contrast, alternative assessment instruments, such as portfolios, utilize an untimed free-response format, in which the answers are open-ended and creative.

Besides portfolios, there are many types of alternative assessment instruments. Portfolios are indeed the most common type of alternative assessment used by content area teachers, but there are two other types that content area teachers also employ in their classes: performance assessments and curriculum-based measurement. All three types include checklists, rubrics, student self-assessment, peer assessment, interviews, and journals.

Checklists are often used to provide evidence of whether a specific criterion or characteristic is present in order to keep track of students' progress over time. For example, let us suppose that in a social studies class in North Carolina, the focus of the unit is on general immigration patterns in the United States. The students, both ELL and non-ELLs, are required to make contact with someone who has recently immigrated to North Carolina, interview him or her, and report back to the class. In their oral report, the students have to describe the background of the person they interviewed (sex, age, place of birth, occupation), explain the reasons for coming to North Carolina and not any other state, and describe at least one challenge that the interviewee has had to deal with in North Carolina. In addition, the students are told that they will have to speak for at least four minutes and that they may not simply read to the class from their notes. A checklist for this social studies activity might look like the one shown in Figure 20.

Figure 20.   Checklist for Social Studies Activity

Presentation Elements	Yes	No
Interviewee's sex		
Interviewee's age		
Interviewee's place of birth		
Interviewee's occupation		
Explains the reasons for immigration		
Describes at least one challenge		
Speaks for a minimum of 4 minutes		
Not reading to class		

The Characteristics of Alternative Assessment Approaches

Some fundamental differences between traditional and alternative means of assessment have been noted. Anderson (1998) examines the two approaches in assessment and finds that they have very different underlying philosophical beliefs and theoretical assumptions, as outlined in Figure 21.

Traditional assessment assumes that knowledge has a single consensual meaning, whereas alternative assessment proposes that it is impossible to reach a consensus about meaning because meaning is based on diverse individual interpretations. In traditional assessment, learning is conceptualized as being passive and individual. Learners (the novices) are *tabulae rasae* (blank slates) who are going to be filled by what the teacher (the expert) considers to constitute knowledge. In addition, the focus of traditional assessment is on individual student performance. Collaboration with others is strictly forbidden, which fosters a competitive environment that emphasizes the outcome at the expense of the process. In alternative assessment, on the other hand, the students search for new meanings and are encouraged to produce instead of reproduce knowledge. Teachers and students are co-learners, and in this environment collaborative learning is encouraged and valued.

Traditional learning considers the product to be more important than the process, and students are evaluated with a test at the end of an instructional cycle. These final outcomes are considered to be representative evidence of the students' learning, and the *how* and *why* are not taken into account. Alternative assessment values both process and product; the *what*, *how*, and *why* are equally important. In terms of focus, traditional assessment concentrates on mastering discrete pieces of information, which essentially represent less critical thinking skills. In contrast, alternative assessment focuses on developing problem-solving skills through inquiry.

The purpose of traditional assessment is to document learning and to create a system that classifies and ranks students. Alternative assessment, on the other hand, assumes that the purpose of assessment is to facilitate learning and not just to classify students as those who mastered the content and those who did not. Traditional assessment focuses almost exclusively on cognitive abilities, and little attention is paid to the students' dispositions to use the skills and strategies that have been taught. Alternative assessment acknowledges a connection between different types of abilities and recognizes that it is pointless to assess student abilities if these abilities are not connected to valued goals.

Figure 21.   The Underlying Philosophical Beliefs and Theoretical Assumptions of the Two Assessment Approaches

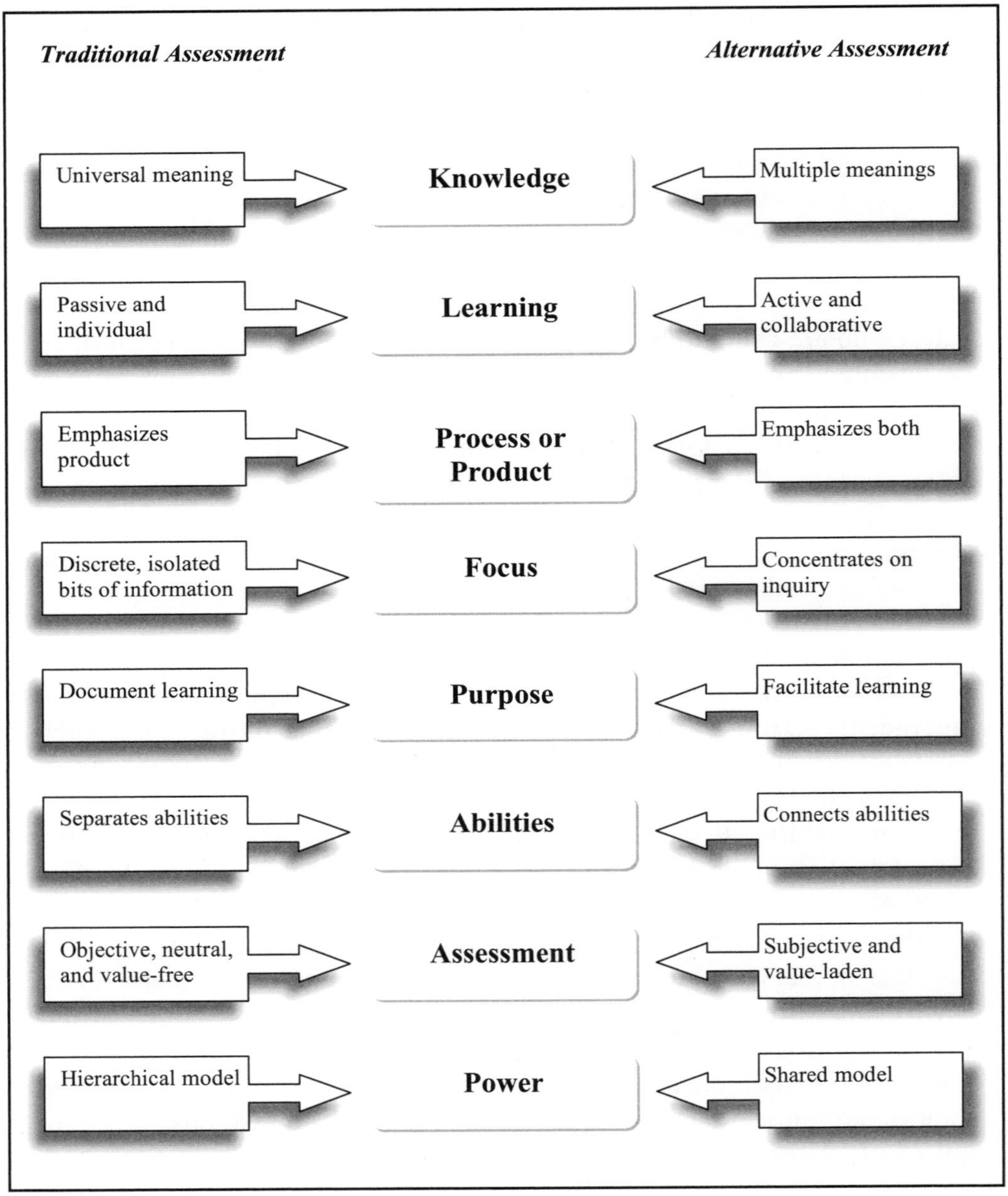

Traditional Assessment   *Alternative Assessment*

Universal meaning	→	**Knowledge**	←	Multiple meanings
Passive and individual	→	**Learning**	←	Active and collaborative
Emphasizes product	→	**Process or Product**	←	Emphasizes both
Discrete, isolated bits of information	→	**Focus**	←	Concentrates on inquiry
Document learning	→	**Purpose**	←	Facilitate learning
Separates abilities	→	**Abilities**	←	Connects abilities
Objective, neutral, and value-free	→	**Assessment**	←	Subjective and value-laden
Hierarchical model	→	**Power**	←	Shared model

The whole concept of assessment, in the traditional sense, is viewed as objective, neutral, and value-free. The assumption is that facts and values are distinct constructs that can be measured objectively and reliably. Alternative assessment embraces a very different point of view, that educational decisions in instruction and assessment are subjective and value-laden. Value systems such as cultural norms influence assessment design at a fundamental level by selecting what questions are going to be asked and what questions are going to be omitted in the assessment instrument.

Finally, in traditional assessment, teachers and school administrators have the power to decide the content of both the curriculum and the assessment. In many instances, students and parents do not participate in this decision-making process, which has important educational consequences. However, in alternative assessment, the assumption is that teachers and other decision makers should share the power with students and parents to make decisions about what is to be learned and assessed, thus utilizing a cooperative model of power instead of the traditional hierarchical one.

The Types of Alternative Assessment

Many content area teachers are not limiting the assessment of their ELLs' progress to traditional methods such as tests and quizzes. They systematically use rubrics, checklists, interviews, and other methods in their evaluations. This section will analyze the three most common types of alternative assessment: performance assessment, curriculum-based measurement, and portfolios. All three types include all the alternative assessment instruments mentioned previously, such as rubrics and interviews.

Performance Assessment

Performance assessment requires students to demonstrate their knowledge in a content area by using a constructed-response format, which means creating a product or engaging in an activity with a measurable outcome (Pierce, 2002). In science, for example, performance assessments include laboratory practical examinations, which entail a direct interaction among students, materials, and lab equipment.

There are both advantages and disadvantages to performance assessment. An advantage is that activities that are less language-bound are more likely to reveal what ELLs know and can do. However, simply changing the assessment method does not mean that linguistic and cultural bias is completely and automatically eliminated. Potential problems are the exclusion of topics that are relevant to ELLs, the dependence on language proficiency in content area assessment response formats, and the use of outside test raters and examiners who are not aware of the cultural and linguistic differences between ELLs and their English-proficient peers (Garcia & Pearson, 1994).

An example of performance assessment in a science class is provided by Shaw (1997). The assessment, called the Rate of Cooling (ROC) Performance Assessment, is a four-day assessment based on the concept of heat transfer and approached by means of a comparative study of the insulation property of different fabrics. The ROC main question is "Given a choice of jackets made from three different materials (A, B, and C), which one would keep you the warmest?"

On the first day, the students work in groups and explore the question. On the second day, they work individually and create an experiment on paper. The prompt for this activity is:

Think about the problem you worked on yesterday. Write down an experiment that can be used to investigate this problem. Your experiment should have a series of numbered steps. These steps should describe the procedure in detail. You may use drawings to help make your experiment as clear as possible. Answer in complete sentences.

On the third day, the students return to their groups to conduct a cooling experiment with the best solution. The chart shown in Figure 22 can be used to record their data.

Figure 22.   Chart for Cooling Experiment

Time (in seconds)	Fabric A Temperature in Celsius	Fabric B Temperature in Celsius	Fabric C Temperature in Celsius
Initial (0 seconds)			
30			
60			
90			
120			
150			
180			

On the fourth day, the students organize their data individually, as requested by this prompt:

Graph the results you got during the cooling experiment for Fabric A, Fabric B, and Fabric C. The temperatures for all three types of fabric should be displayed on a single axis in a clear, easy to understand manner. Use a different color for each fabric data.

Based on the information collected during the experiments, the students are required to answer the main question of ROC, which is:

Given a choice of jackets made from three different materials, which one would keep you the warmest: Fabric A, Fabric B, or Fabric C? Give *specific evidence* to support your answer. You may use graphs or drawings to support your answer. Answer in complete sentences.

At the end of the activity, science teachers may use the rubric shown in Table 16 to score the final product, which is represented by the answer to the question stated above.

Performance assessment is very effective in measuring ELLs' abilities and skills in real-life tasks and situations. The assessment tasks and materials can vary to accommodate ELLs' individual academic development and lan-

Table 16.   Rubric for Science Experiment

Level	Description
4 — Exceeds expectation	Correctly identifies Fabric A. Supporting evidence is clear, specific, and concrete. Supporting evidence is based on the student graph. Supporting evidence includes a comparison of the fabrics.
3 — Meets expectation	Correctly identifies Fabric A. Supporting evidence is only slightly unclear. Supporting evidence may be based on the student graph. Supporting evidence may include a comparison of the fabrics.
2 — Approaches expectation	Correctly identifies Fabric A. Supporting evidence is inaccurate, incomplete, or unclear or may be lacking completely.
1 — Does not approach expectation	Incorrectly identifies Fabric B or C. There is no supporting evidence.
0 — No response	No fabric is identified.

guage proficiency levels. Losardo and Notari-Syverson (2001) identify several advantages as well as several limitations of using performance assessment.

One of the most important advantages is that performance assessment focuses on a student's strengths, or what an ELL can do. It enables content area teachers to understand the reasons for a specific academic measurement outcome by providing in-depth information on various aspects of the performance, such as the type of strategies employed during the assessment, the errors made during the process, and the errors in the final product.

Another advantage of performance assessment is the meaningful context in which it occurs. Samples collected though assessment are a direct and accurate reflection of what the students can actually do, and they provide valuable evidence that is often neglected in more traditional assessments.

Nevertheless, performance assessment also has its limitations. One is the lack of standardization and evaluation criteria. Performance assessment is inherently complex and difficult to quantify. This type of assessment is based on real-life situations that involve multifaceted tasks in which a number of academic skills are measured in an integrated manner.

Another limitation is that performance assessment requires a high level of expertise. Content-area teachers who employ this assessment method have to develop meaningful tasks and determine clear criteria for evaluation. If teachers are not familiar with assessment and curriculum practices, they might find it very difficult to implement this type of assessment in their content area classrooms.

Curriculum-Based Measurement

Curriculum-based measurement (CBM) is a set of procedures for assessing student performance on long-term curriculum goals in various content areas. Deno (1992) states that CBM is an objective and continuing measurement of student outcomes that is conducted to improve instructional planning and effectively evaluate academic objectives. Furthermore, CBM results should be used to create a database for each student in order to allow the teacher to evaluate the effectiveness of instruction by identifying whether curriculum goals have been met.

To accomplish the evaluation of curriculum goals, teachers in the content areas can develop CBM tests called *probes*, which are based on the curriculum material that ELLs are expected to master by the end of an instructional cycle, usually a semester or an academic year. These probes are administered to ELLs once or twice a week, and the scores are recorded on a graph. The graph can then be used to identify ELLs' growth within an instructional program and to identify which areas of the curriculum should be revisited by the content area teachers. CBM may therefore be used to provide measurable descriptors of academic behavior of ELLs in the content areas. The CBM results help teachers to assess the effectiveness of their instruction by measuring their ELLs' progress.

Here are four examples of math curriculum-based measurement (M-CBM) probes for first grade ELLs, adapted here from Clarke and Shinn (2004). These examples of M-CBM are based on assessing number-sense development. Students who have number sense have the ability to understand the meaning of numbers and the relationship among them (Commission on Standards for School Mathematics, 1989). The curriculum objective of number sense for first grade students can potentially be assessed through at least four M-CBM probes: number identification, oral counting, missing number, and quantity discrimination.

One kind of number-identification probe requires ELLs to orally identify numbers between 0 and 20. ELLs are given a sheet of randomly selected numbers formatted in a grid, as shown in Figure 23.

ELLs are asked to orally identify the numbers of the grid from left to right or from top to bottom. The math teacher counts the numbers that are correctly identified in one minute. When ELLs struggle or hesitate more than three seconds in the process of identification, the math teacher tells them to try the next number. After the assessment, the math teacher records the performance on a graph. The same probe can be administered in subsequent weeks, and the results will show if ELLs have the skill of correctly identifying numbers at the end of the instructional cycle.

The probe exemplified should be used with caution by math teachers because it requires ELLs to rely heavily on their possibly underdeveloped oral academic skills in English. The next probe described may be more appropriate for an ELL who has previously had math instruction in his or her native language. For this particular probe, which is a written-counting M-CBM, ELLs are asked to write numbers, starting from one, sequentially in one min-

Figure 23.   Worksheet for Number-Identification Probe

1	3	10	6	7	16	3
9	11	5	2	19	10	20
13	14	19	4	15	1	17
5	2	6	8	20	5	11
18	15	7	1	13	19	4
8	12	20	18	13	16	7
3	14	4	12	17	20	9

ute. Their responses can be tallied by the math teacher using the form shown in Figure 24.

If math instruction has been conducted in English and the ELLs have had no previous schooling experience in math, the probe can be changed into an oral-counting M-CBM. Instead of writing the numbers, the ELLs are asked to count orally, starting from one, in one minute. The assessment rubric is the same as that used for the written-counting M-CBM. If the ELLs stop or hesitate for more than six seconds to say a number, the math teacher instructs them to say the next number.

A typical missing-number probe requires ELLs to name the missing number from a string of numbers from 0 to 20. The ELLs are given a work sheet with boxes that contain strings of three numbers in which the first, the middle, or the last number in the string missing, as shown in Figure 25.

The ELLs are given one minute to orally state the number that is missing. The math teacher counts the correct answers and graphs them for comparison with other times that this probe is administered during the academic year. When the ELLs stop or hesitate for more than three seconds to say a number, the math teacher instructs them to move to the next set of numbers.

Number-sense development for ELLs can be also assessed though a quantity-discrimination probe. This M-CBM asks ELLs to identify orally which of two visually presented numbers is larger. The ELLs are given a sheet like the one in Figure 26 and asked to identify which number is larger in each box.

Figure 24.   Tally Sheet for Written-Counting Probe

Date: _____

Student Name: _____

Number of correctly counted numbers: _____

Number of incorrectly counted numbers: _____

Last number in the sequence: _____

Figure 25.   Worksheet for Missing-Number Probe

4 _ 6	_ 18 19	11 _ 13	6 7 _
18 _ 20	8 9 _	14 15 _	2 3 _
_ 11 12	9 10 _	17 18 _	12 _ 14
_ 16 17	1 2 _	10 11 _	5 _ 7

Figure 26.   Worksheet for Quantity-Discrimination Probe

5 12	2 9	8 7	13 15	20 11
4 2	3 1	11 15	16 19	9 1
20 19	16 17	15 18	3 7	4 1
3 2	12 13	4 9	7 10	12 11
11 19	10 20	7 2	15 10	6 7

Only the correct answers are marked, and if the ELLs stop or hesitate for more than three seconds to say a number, the math teacher instructs them to move to the next box on the work sheet.

Content area teachers should use CBM with ELLs for two reasons. First, CBM is very easy to administer and score, and it requires only one to three minutes of class time once or twice a week. Second, the results of a CBM can be compiled into a database to determine if ELLs are making progress in the context of the instruction they are receiving. If the ELLs show that they have not yet mastered a critical skill, the content area teachers can modify their teaching to meet the needs of this student population. Research has shown that instructors who use CBM to evaluate their instructional effectiveness usually have students who achieve higher grades than do teachers who do not use CBM (Hosp & Hosp, 2003).

Portfolios

Portfolios are perhaps the most popular alternative assessment instruments in K–12 settings in the United States. Grosvenor (1993) defines a portfolio as a record of learning that is a reflection of students' work. The material that is collected shows a student's progress toward educational objectives and is a result of the collaborative effort between the student and the teacher.

O'Malley and Pierce (1996) identify three main types of portfolios: working portfolios, display portfolios, and assessment portfolios. A working portfolio contains a collection of work that is in progress as well as work that has been completed. The main purpose of a working portfolio is to serve as a storage space for student work. The materials that are collected here may be selected for either a display or an assessment portfolio.

A display (or showcase) portfolio is composed of materials that demonstrate a student's highest level of achievement. Most of the items in a display portfolio are selected from the working portfolio. However, it is not unusual for students to include work that has been completed outside the classroom, such as a project completed in an after-school program. The students are the ones who decide what are the best pieces of work that will illustrate who they are and what they can do.

An assessment portfolio includes materials that document what students have learned during a semester or a year. The content of the curriculum is the main criterion that students use for their selection of the materials. For example, if the curriculum requires mathematical problem solving and mathematical communication, the assessment portfolio will have to include entries that document both problem solving and communication.

In developing portfolios in content area classes, teachers should look at both the process and the product. The development process is essential to a successful and effective portfolio. Therefore, it is imperative for content area teachers to follow a very well-defined model when they want to use portfolios in their assessment of English language learners.

The development model, illustrated in Figure 27, focuses on both process and product. The process consists of four basic steps: purpose, collection, selection, and reflection. Once the portfolio is created, the focus shifts to the product, which has to be assessed by the instructor. Based on this assessment, the teacher provides feedback to the student and the parents and uses the assessment information to inform instruction.

Purpose

Content area teachers should decide what the purpose of the portfolio is before they start collecting materials from their students. For example, for an assessment portfolio, the materials to be collected should focus on documenting whether the student has attained the curricular goals and objectives. A typical assessment portfolio for an ELL in a middle school math class should include assignments that show the student's ability to create and interpret graphs or to solve complex math problems. Once the purpose has been established, the task of collecting the materials becomes targeted to fulfilling that purpose.

Figure 27.   A Portfolio Development Model

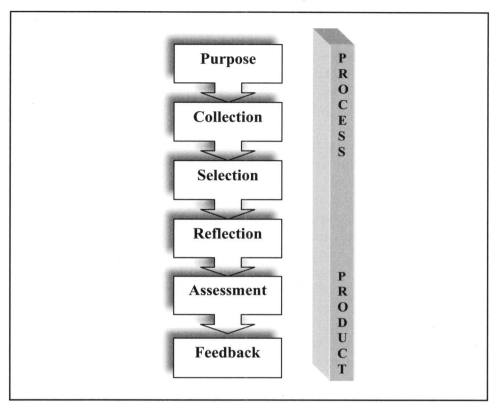

Collection

Once the purpose of the portfolio has been established, the teacher and the ELLs can start collecting the work to be included. Traditionally, after the students receive feedback from their teacher, they usually discard their work. Therefore, it is important for teachers to realize that they must explicitly show ELLs the steps that are involved in the collection process and then model the process, especially for students who are LEP.

In addition, a content-are teacher should allow ELLs ample opportunities to try out these steps before the actual collection process begins. During the collection process, the teacher should remember that not all work that is assigned to the students is to be saved and collected. Classroom assignments such as work sheets might not be appropriate for a portfolio. Collection of materials should stop when there is sufficient material that clearly and thoroughly illustrates that the ELLs have attained the instructional objectives.

Selection

When enough work has been collected, the ELLs and their teacher should decide which pieces of work will be included in the portfolio, according to the already established purpose of the portfolio. For example, for a display portfolio, the ELLs will select their best pieces of work, without relying too much on the learning objectives as a principal selection criterion. In other words, the selected pieces reflect who the students are and what they think is important to them as individuals. On the other hand, for an assessment portfolio, the main criterion is very different. In this case the selected pieces should be the best reflection of the mastery of the learning objectives that are stated in the academic curriculum.

In terms of quantity, there is no set number of items for each type of portfolio. For an assessment portfolio, the number of selected items should unequivocally show attainment of the learning objectives. For a display portfolio, the number will probably be established by the teacher, who will most likely consider space or time constraints (e.g., the students will select their three best papers from a semester to reflect their best work in science, instead of their 10 or 20 best papers, which would require more space for storing and more time for selection).

Reflection

After the selection process is over, the ELLs move to the fourth stage in the development process, reflection. During this stage, the students articulate their thinking, in writing or in one-to-one conferences with their teachers, about each item in the portfolio. Through reflection, ELLs become aware of themselves as learners and get a better image of their strengths in terms of their knowledge of the content area.

Assessment

Once the portfolio is assembled, it is assessed. Danielson and Abrutyn (1997) propose several recommendations for grading portfolios. Their first recommendation is that grades should be assigned only to an assessment portfolio, because display portfolio reflects a student's own definition and judgment of high-quality work, and a working portfolio only stores student work for the assessment portfolio and it is not a finished, ready-to-be evaluated product.

Their second recommendation is that each item in an assessment portfolio should be evaluated against clear criteria, using a scoring guide that the ELLs have helped to create. Then the assessment portfolio should also be assessed as a whole for completeness and organization. The criteria and performance levels for this should be clearly articulated and made available to ELLs in advance so that the students have an opportunity to learn and practice the required skills for completeness and organization. Figure 28 is an example of a grading rubric for evaluating the growth and achievement of ELLs in a science classroom.

Feedback

The results of a portfolio assessment are used to communicate information to ELLs about their academic progress, to show ELLs' growth to their parents, and to design future instruction for ELLs. Because of the importance of portfolios in determining the extent of student progress, research recommends active student involvement in the assessment procedures.

Active participation in the assessment of their portfolios strengthens ELLs' cognitive and metacognitive awareness of the learning process, and it can also encourage ELLs' self-determination in learning, which has positive

Figure 28.   Grading Rubric for Science Portfolios

Evaluation Criterion: *Growth and achievement*

Definition: The student shows improvement in and development of a variety of concepts and skills.

Level of Achievement	Description
4 — Exceeds expectation	Shows excellent performance consistently or continued performance improvement.
3 — Meets expectation	Shows good performance with general improvement or consistency in performance.
2 — Approaches expectation	Shows little good performance with many inconsistencies.
1 — Does not approach expectation	Shows worsening performance over time or completely inconsistent performance.
0 — No response or unacceptable	No response or no attempt made to illustrate growth and achievement.

effects on their learning (Moya & O'Malley, 1994). One way in which active ELL participation in the assessment process can be achieved is to ask the students to arrange their work from the most to the least effective and to answer questions (orally or in writing) about the qualities of each selection, the processes and strategies that were employed in the creation of each selection, and the reasons that the less effective pieces were not as successful as the more effective ones. Both students and parents also can benefit tremendously from the results of portfolios and their assessment. These results provide detailed examples of the students' skills and interests, a critical dimension that traditional grades fail to deliver.

Because portfolios provide a more authentic and comprehensive image of content area knowledge achievement, teachers can use the information from portfolios to improve teaching effectiveness. When teachers use portfolios in their classrooms, they tend to move toward a more learner-centered model of instruction, which encourages the students to take more responsibility for their own learning. Portfolios also provide critical information on the areas in which ELLs have still not achieved mastery of content, and this allows the teachers to revisit and reteach that content for the current students and to emphasize it in future classes.

The Challenges of Alternative Assessment

Many educational practitioners consider alternative assessments such as portfolios, rubrics, and student self-evaluations to be more authentic and more valid than the more widely used traditional pencil-and-paper tests for measuring ELLs' content area knowledge. Portfolios are reflective of an ELL's work and performance during regular classroom activities that are directly connected to the curriculum. As a result, the materials collected for a portfolio are documentation of actual curriculum goals and objectives.

Portfolios are also individualized for each ELL and emphasize multiple methods of evaluation by allowing multiple ways of documenting ELLs' work. This variety in materials provides a comprehensive picture of ELLs' actual level of competence in a content area. Portfolio assessment also encourages ELLs to participate in the assessment and learning process by allowing them to select the materials in the portfolio and to evaluate their own work. This active participation promotes communication, language-development, problem-solving, and metacognitive skills.

Thus, with all these educational advantages, why do states not use portfolio assessment, or any other type of alternative assessment for the content areas, more extensively? Why do they still rely on large-scale standardized tests to measure ELLs' achievement in academic knowledge?

Gomez (1999) identifies several challenges of the use of assessment portfolios with ELLS. First, portfolios are difficult to reduce to a single score or set of scores. Instead of a simple score or grade, portfolio evaluation often consists of a narrative that describes the strengths and weaknesses of the final product. Because words and not numbers are used, it is more difficult to use portfolios for comparing the performances of students in different districts or from year to year.

Another challenge results from the difficulty of ensuring standardized testing conditions. With assessment portfolios, there is the possibility of considerable variation in the amount of support that teachers provide to students, in the amount of time that students spend on portfolio samples, and in the extent of the help that students get from outside sources. This variation in performance conditions raises serious questions about the validity of assessment portfolios.

Cost can be added to the list of challenges of assessment portfolios. Designing and implementing portfolios requires extensive amounts of time in order to align the assessment task to the curriculum and to develop sound scoring criteria and reliable scoring tools. Scoring itself can pose a serious challenge to districts and states that would like to develop and implement assessment portfolios. For ELLs, scoring should take into account how to measure not only content knowledge but also language proficiency. That takes time and resources, which are always in short supply in the education field. Therefore, it is very difficult to design scoring rubrics for all learners without raising questions about validity and practicality.

Recognizing that traditional standardized tests may not be appropriate for students who are LEP, some states have attempted to implement portfolio-based assessment approaches for ELLs. In 1999, Wisconsin started practicing a portfolio assessment for ELLs to test academic content areas that were part of the state accountability system. Shortly after that, Arkansas, Delaware, the District of Columbia, Rhode Island, and Vermont formed a consortium to develop an assessment similar to the one developed in Wisconsin (Zehr, 2003).

However, in 2006, Arkansas and Wisconsin decided not to use their large-scale portfolio-based assessments any longer, after receiving letters from the U.S. Department of Education that required them to prove that those assessments were valid. Indiana also stopped the use of an alternative test for ELLs that was based on portfolios and teacher observations. The U.S. Department of Education did, however, approve an alternative test for ELLs in North Carolina that has a portfolio component. This federally approved alternative assessment is a checklist that is based on teacher observations and a portfolio of student work (Zehr, 2006).

What can the states do to make sure that their portfolios and other alternative assessment approaches are valid and reliable instruments for measuring the achievement of ELLs in the content areas? The model presented in Figure 29 illustrates the steps that educational practitioners should follow in designing, implementing, and evaluating valid and reliable assessment portfolios.

At the *design* stage, the stakeholders at the school, district, and state levels decide on the goal and purpose of assessment by portfolio. Once the general direction has been established, a development task force is set up that should include ESL and content area teachers, school administrators, and parents. Based on statewide standards and curriculum, the task force decides what the goals for ELL learning performance are and how these goals are to be assessed. A list of what materials the assessment portfolio should contain is developed, as well as clear and comprehensive scoring rubrics and checklists. After the portfolio guidelines and scoring instruments are developed, the program should be pilot-tested for one or two school years. Based on feedback from teachers who use and score the assessment portfolios, the effectiveness of the portfolio program is to assessed, with a special emphasis on the performance of ELLs.

At the *implementation* stage, after the program has been found to assess both language and content development for ELLs, the assessment portfolios are administered throughout the district or the state. Clear guidelines for implementation must be developed in advance in order to standardize the assessment procedure as much as possible, in terms of the time, the place,

**Figure 29.   A Model for Creating Large-Scale
Assessment Portfolios for ELLs**

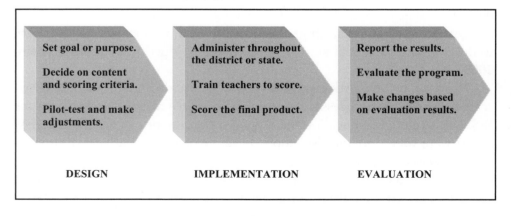

DESIGN	IMPLEMENTATION	EVALUATION
Set goal or purpose. Decide on content and scoring criteria. Pilot-test and make adjustments.	Administer throughout the district or state. Train teachers to score. Score the final product.	Report the results. Evaluate the program. Make changes based on evaluation results.

and the manner in which student work samples are to be gathered. Once the portfolios are collected, the teachers will be trained to score them, using well-defined scoring criteria that take into account the language proficiency of ELLs. At the end of the training session, the teachers will score the portfolios, usually at one location over several days.

At the *evaluation* stage, the results are disseminated to the students, the teachers, the administrators, and the parents. After one year of administration throughout the district or the school, the effectiveness of the program is evaluated. The assessment portfolio system should be changed if that is deemed necessary, based on feedback from ELLs, teachers, and parents.

Things to Consider

- Alternative assessments in content area classrooms are useful with ELLs because of the multidimensional perspective of student progress and depth of academic knowledge they provide.

- Content-area alternative assessments should be based on curricular standards and should be an integral part of the instructional flow when teachers decide to use them.

- When developing alternative assessments, content area teachers should make a distinction between assessing content knowledge and language proficiency.

- Alternative assessments should pass the test of quality just like traditional assessments, meaning that they need to be valid and reliable.

- Before content area teacher develop these type of assessments, they should be remember the main disadvantages of alternative assessments: they are not easy to administer and score and they are time consuming. Taking these disadvantages into account at the design stage will make alternative assessments more practical and easier to administer.

Chapter 6

Essential Considerations in Assessing English Language Learners

We have examined both large-scale and classroom-based assessments for measuring content area knowledge for ELLS. We have looked at how effective the test accommodations in large-scale assessments are, and we have offered several solutions for designing better and more effective tests, not only for statewide standardized tests but also for classroom-based assessments that are developed by content area teachers who have limited knowledge of second-language acquisition processes and applied linguistics.

In this chapter we will examine three essential practices that content area educators should remember when assessing ELLs, and we will also include several concluding remarks.

Three "Must-Do" ELL Assessment Practices for Content Area Educators

The following recommendations are based on the research on ELL assessment and represent a very basic set of practices. First, content area educators should make sure that their assessment of ELLs is a direct reflection of their content area instructional activities. Second, content area teachers should make sure that they are testing content, not language, by reducing the language barrier, especially in areas such as math, science, and social studies. Third, content area educators should know what accommodations are allowed in their state and then use them in their classroom-based assessments in order to make sure that their ELLs can take full advantage of them on large-scale tests.

1. Make Sure That Assessment Reflects Content Area Instruction

It is very important that classroom assessment be based on classroom activities, which in turn must be based on objectives that are derived from curricular standards. All states have some form of large-scale content area tests that are based on statewide curricular standards. Content area teachers should never teach to the test, but they have to make sure that classroom instruction and the subsequent activities will cover the content that will be tested by the state tests. It is not recommended that a teacher consistently create completely different learning objectives for their ELLs, but rather that all classroom objectives fit each ELL student's level of English language proficiency. Just as tests should be direct reflections of classroom objectives, so too should adapted classroom objectives be assessed by using adapted tests.

Content-area teachers should not introduce a new test task to ELLs on the test day; all test tasks should reflect activities that have already been introduced in an instructional setting multiple times. This type of transparency and established routine is critical, so that ELLs are assessed on their knowledge of content, not on their knowledge of how to do the activity. For example, some ELLs may consider a short-answer response to consist of three or four words, whereas the usual expectation of a short-answer task is the equivalent of at least two or three linked sentences. If ELLs are asked to produce short-answer responses on a test, and they are not aware that they are expected to produce a full paragraph, they will not be able to demonstrate full mastery of the content because their understanding of the task is different from that of the teacher.

2. Reduce the Language Barrier

Teachers of math, science, and social studies must understand that they should create assessments that focus primarily on assessing content and not on measuring English language proficiency. It is thus critical to know how to create assessments that match ELLs' level of English language development. The TESOL standards described in Chapter 4, as well as the assessment activities proposed in Appendix A, represent a very good resource for content area teachers who may feel lost when they need to design assessment activities for their ELLs in content area classrooms.

Visuals and graphic organizers are essential tools within most classrooms. Teachers should use the same visuals and graphic organizers on tests that were used in classroom instruction, in order to help reduce the language requirements of content tests. Moreover, visuals and graphics should appear in similar positions on tests as in classroom activities. For example, if a T-diagram has been used in a classroom activity to compare two objects or concepts, the teacher should not switch to a Venn diagram on a test to compare two objects or concepts.

Finally, there is the issue of test translations into an ELL's native language. Research has found at least three major problems with this strategy. First, identical translations are almost impossible, simply because word difficulty and other procedures rarely have a one-to-one correspondence in all languages (Figueroa, 1990). Second, if the language of instruction has been English, it is unlikely that an ELL will be familiar with the content in his or her native language. Only when ELLs are taught content bilingually should they be expected to demonstrate the knowledge learned in English in their native language. Third, ELLs may not be literate in their native language. Testing in Spanish, for example, can be considered valid only if the Spanish-speaking students can read and write at an appropriate level in that language.

3. Use State-Approved Accommodations

All states allow test accommodations for ELLs in statewide large-scale assessments. An accommodation is effective if it levels the playing field for ELLs. Therefore, content area teachers should make a point of using state-sanctioned accommodations in their classroom-based assessments and especially on their classroom-based tests.

The first step in putting these accommodations into practice is for teachers to become familiar with what accommodation policies their states allow for content area tests. Chapter 3 provided a very detailed state-by-state description of these policies. Once the state-authorized accommodations are identified, content area teachers should do two things: They should adapt ELL accommodations to the demands and characteristics of their classrooms, and they should emphasize the accommodations that best reduce the language barrier for their ELLs.

Conclusion

What is the most reliable, valid, and practical approach in assessing ELLs? Because legislation demands the integration of language proficiency with content mastery, it is not possible to construct a reliable picture of ELLs' achievement in the content areas by relying on one approach only, either traditional or alternative. Prior chapters showed that norm-referenced tests often do not provide an accurate indication of the level of content area achievement of ELLs, simply because this population is not adequately reflected in the standardization sample. On the other hand, alternative assessments have their own challenges. Even though they might provide a better picture of ELLs' content mastery, portfolios and other performance assessments are limited in their application to other settings and in making comparisons of students.

Thus, it is important for educational practitioners to remember that both traditional and alternative assessments have their own limitations; neither is the perfect assessment approach in terms of the assessment principles discussed in Chapter 2. Rather, both approaches should be integrated in a comprehensive model of academic achievement assessment that should be based primarily on the unique characteristics of each ELL.

Therefore, the method of assessment that is the most appropriate for ELLs should be selected only after individual cultural, language, and schooling experiences have been identified and evaluated. Accountability is here to stay, but educators should make sure that this increased trend toward constant measurement of student achievement does not alienate the growing population of ELLs or deprive them of educational opportunities.

Things to Consider

- Content area teachers need to understand the process and stages of acquiring a second language in order to accurately interpret the language proficiency ELLs in English.

- When possible, ELLs should be assessed in the home language as well as English. Knowing the social and academic language proficiency of ELLs in their home language is a key element for long-term academic success and educational planning. When assessment instruments are not available in the ELLs' native language, dynamic assessment methods can provide information on the ELLs' content knowledge and language abilities.

- Parents and other family members should be included in the assessment process. Parents can be reliable sources of information about their child's language and overall development (Pavri & Fowler, 2005). Parents have the ability to share crucial information about ELLs language ability when communicating with siblings, peers, parents, and other adults.

Assessment Activities for Mathematics, Science, and Social Studies,
Adapted from the TESOL Proficiency Levels

Content area teachers who need to develop assessment instruments for their ELLs can use the following assessment activities as a guide. After they find out the English language level proficiency of their ELLs, they can choose for their assessment various topics selected from their content areas, such as math or science. Additionally, the list of assessment activities gives them the option of focusing on one of the four language skills, making the assessment more targeted and relevant in the results obtained.

Mathematics

Topics Grades Pre-K–K	Geometry, dimensions	Time	Patterns	Numbers, operations
Language Domains	Reading	Writing	Listening	Speaking
Level 1, Starting	Match pictures with realia in small groups.	Draw pictures to express time of day.	Imitate pattern sounds (clap, snap) in groups.	Count up to 10 objects with a partner, using number words.
Level 2, Emerging	Order pictures or realia (e.g., from big to small).	Draw and write (letters and scribble writing) about morning, noon, and night.	Identify patterns in the environment based on oral descriptions.	Repeat choral chants involving addition and subtraction.
Level 3, Developing	Label pictures (rectangle, triangle, circle) according to measurable characteristics.	Draw and write (letters, scribble writing, and invented spelling) about special times of day.	Put illustrations in sequence or group them according to patterns, following oral directions.	Describe the relationship between two objects (e.g., which one is bigger, which one is smaller).
Level 4, Expanding	Find matching shape words from print sources.	Create a short story about an event with a partner or in groups, using drawings, words, and invented spelling.	Form simple patterns with a partner, using manipulatives, following oral directions.	Ask classmates comparative questions involving addition and subtraction.
Level 5, Bridging	Find words for shapes, order, and position from print sources.	Construct illustrated stories about events, using drawings, words, invented spelling, and phrases.	Form extended patterns, using manipulatives, following oral directions.	Talk about math stories, using comparative language.

Topics Grades 1–3	Addition, subtraction, multiplication	Shapes	Time	Estimation, money
Language Domains	Reading	Writing	Listening	Speaking
Level 1, Starting	Identify words associated with symbols for addition, subtraction, or multiplication with a partner.	Label shapes found in pictures.	Show or draw on clocks, based on oral directions.	Identify and sort coins, bills, or numerals with a partner.
Level 2, Emerging	Identify and sort phrases associated with symbols for addition, subtraction, or multiplication with a partner.	Make lists of shapes found in everyday life.	Role-play activities based on oral directions and different times of day.	Identify information about prices from pictures or other illustrations with a partner.
Level 3, Developing	Find and categorize by operation phrases and sentences found in illustrated text, with a partner.	Describe features of shapes found in everyday life.	Draw or show on a clock responses to more complex statements or questions about time.	Pretend you are buying or selling merchandise with a partner, using coins and bills.
Level 4, Expanding	Create illustrated stories based on math problems with a partner.	Write paragraphs, using features of shapes found in everyday life.	Solve oral word problems based on time, using visual or graphic support.	Compare prices across the United States, or between the United States and other countries, with a partner.
Level 5, Bridging	Identify clues for problem solving in extended math texts.	Write stories, using features of shapes found in everyday life.	Make inferences from oral math problems found in stories or classroom texts.	Discuss the value of money in the United States and other countries.

Topics Grades 4–5	Three-dimensional shapes, polygons, angles	Data analysis	Patterns, relations, functions	Basic operations
Language Domains	Reading	Writing	Listening	Speaking
Level 1, Starting	Sort figures by characteristics from labeled visuals and objects (four sides, three angles).	Label variables from tables, charts, and graphs with a partner.	Recognize algebraic symbols or elements from oral commands with visual support.	State and confirm math operations represented visually.
Level 2, Emerging	Match characteristics and properties from visuals, objects, and phrases (e.g., *the left angle of the square*).	Formulate and answer questions from tables, charts, and graphs with a partner.	Match phrases to algebraic symbols or elements from visually supported spoken statements.	Relate how to solve problems from provided models with a partner.
Level 3, Developing	Distinguish among figures from text supported by illustrations.	Organize and describe information in tables, charts, and graphs with a partner.	Identify relationships between algebraic symbols or functions according to spoken descriptions with visual support.	Share steps outlined to solve everyday problems with a partner.
Level 4, Expanding	Construct or draw figures by following steps in visually supported text.	Write paragraphs, using information in tables, charts, and graphs.	Sort algebraic math sentences according to spoken descriptions with graphic support.	Give everyday examples of how to solve problems with a partner or in small groups.
Level 5, Bridging	Infer geometric relationships among figures from language-modified grade-level text.	Summarize and apply information in tables, charts, and graphs to new situations.	Analyze change and identify transformation in various contexts from spoken descriptions.	Apply information from solving problems to everyday situations.

Topics Grades 6–8	Data sets and interpretation, plots	Probability, proportion	Metric units, statistics	Area, volume
Language Domains	Reading	Writing	Listening	Speaking
Level 1, Starting	Identify variables and integers in charts and graphs with a partner.	Record outcomes of hands-on math activities.	Identify units of measurement as described orally with visual support.	Name figures from real objects or diagrams.
Level 2, Emerging	Respond to questions based on variables and integers in charts and graphs with a partner.	Estimate outcomes with illustrations and words, using real objects.	Compare and classify units of measurement as described orally with visual support.	Define dimensions of figures based on objects or diagrams, using general language.
Level 3, Developing	Create data sets with a partner based on variables found in texts, plots, charts, and graphs.	Formulate estimates with simple phrases or sentences, using concrete examples.	Construct graphs from oral descriptions, using units of measurement.	Describe the dimensions of figures based on objects or diagrams, using some specialized math language.
Level 4, Expanding	Chart, graph, or plot data sets with a partner, according to written directions.	Compare possible combinations, using graphic organizers and sentences.	Offer solutions to orally presented math problems, using graphic representations.	Analyze figures or operations in real-life situations, using specialized math language.
Level 5, Bridging	Interpret data presented in charts, graphs, and plots.	Explain in a paragraph the use of different combinations.	Evaluate and use various graphic representations to offer solutions to orally presented math problems.	Explain the differences among operations and figures, using specialized math language.

Topics Grades 9–12	Data interpretation	Algebra	Polygons	Problem solving
Language Domains	Reading	Writing	Listening	Speaking
Level 1, Starting	Match graphs from everyday print sources to text with a partner.	Copy and label equations, inequalities, and expressions.	Identify in small groups the properties of figures in visual representations or oral descriptions.	State or repeat steps in problem solving, using manipulatives or visuals.
Level 2, Emerging	Categorize information gathered from graphs with a partner.	Describe simple equations, inequalities, and expressions based on real-life situations with a partner.	Compare and categorize figures in visual representations or oral descriptions with a partner.	Describe steps in problem solving, using tools or technology.
Level 3, Developing	Analyze data from charts, graphs, and tables to draw conclusions with a partner.	Create explanations for equations, inequalities, and expressions with a partner.	Draw or build figures based on oral directions with a partner.	Explain in detail steps in problem solving.
Level 4, Expanding	Organize and interpret data from visually supported texts with a partner.	Provide solutions to equations, inequalities, and expressions in small groups.	Draw or point to figures based on language associated with sides and angles of figures, with a partner.	Show at least two approaches to solving the same math problem in teams.
Level 5, Bridging	Make predictions based on charts and graphs.	Create word problems based on equations, inequalities, and expressions.	Change geometric shapes, following oral directions.	Show examples of various strategies for solving grade-level math problems.

Science

Topics Grades Pre-K–K	Senses	Investigation	Animate and non-animate	Seasons
Language Domains	Reading	Writing	Listening	Speaking
Level 1, Starting	Identify different senses in illustrated books.	Draw or copy pictures based on class activities or observations.	Identify animate and inanimate objects in pictures or realia.	Name objects or pictures associated with the seasons.
Level 2, Emerging	Categorize pictures according to labels and illustrations of the senses.	Make drawings and labels with letters and scribble writing based on class activities. observations	Collect and display pictures and realia based on oral directions.	Describe activities, based on illustrations that are season-specific in one's native country or the United States.
Level 3, Developing	Sort visual representations of activities according to labels and illustration of the senses.	Create a list of materials, using drawings, letters, scribble writing, and invented spelling.	Respond to questions or oral descriptions, using pictures or realia.	Respond to questions about photos or illustrations, describing different seasons.
Level 4, Expanding	Associate sensory responses with scenes in picture books.	Describe necessary steps of investigation, using drawings and words or phrases with invented spelling.	Sort and match characteristics according to pictures and oral directions.	Compare and contrast characteristics of the seasons, using photos and illustrations.
Level 5, Bridging	Compare information in picture books about the senses.	Write stories about class experiments, using drawings and words or phrases with invented spelling.	Arrange pictures of living beings based on observable features, described orally.	Talk about likes and dislikes about the seasons.

Topics Grades 1–3	Cycles, living creatures in the environment	Plants, animals	The stars and the sky	Movement
Language Domains	Reading	Writing	Listening	Speaking
Level 1, Starting	Match pictures with labels.	Draw and label plants and animals from pictures or real-life observations.	Draw objects in the sky from models and pictures, following oral directions.	Name materials and supplies required to study familiar moving objects, with a partner.
Level 2, Emerging	Match pictures with phases in cycles.	Draw and describe plants and animals from pictures or real-life observations.	Draw and position objects in the sky from maps or models following oral directions.	List uses for materials and supplies required to study moving objects, ith a partner.
Level 3, Developing	Draw or choose responses to illustrated paragraphs about stages in cycles.	Compare physical characteristics of plants and animals from pictures or real-life observations, using graphic support.	Locate objects in the sky from maps or videos, following oral descriptions.	State the steps required to study moving objects, with a partner.
Level 4, Expanding	Categorize multiparagraph text according to illustrated phases of processes.	Write notes or paragraphs about plants and animals from experiences or real-life observations.	Make a distinction among objects in the sky from videos or maps, following oral descriptions.	Follow the steps required to study moving objects and discuss the results with a partner.
Level 5, Bridging	Identify relevant information about various cycles and apply it to new contexts.	Write journal or learning log entries about plants and animals from experiences or real-life observations.	Define relationships among objects in the sky from oral descriptions.	Explain the results of studying moving objects, with a partner.

Topics Grades 4–5	Matter and energy	The solar system	Health and body	Natural phenomena
Language Domains	Reading	Writing	Listening	Speaking
Level 1, Starting	Select examples of forms of energy from print (billboards, newspapers).	Draw the planets of the solar system based on labeled representations or models.	Match health and body words with labels on diagrams, following oral directions.	Name natural phenomena, using pictures and illustrations.
Level 2, Emerging	Arrange steps of energy use, using phrases and illustrations.	Make notes on the solar system from videos and illustrations.	Select examples of body parts from visuals, following oral directions.	Describe natural phenomena, using pictures and illustrations.
Level 3, Developing	Test hypotheses about energy, following illustrated directions.	Compare features of the solar system from models, videos, or pictures, using a graphic organizer.	Create displays, using visuals of body parts, organs, and systems, following oral descriptions.	Identify characteristics of natural phenomena, using pictures and illustrations.
Level 4, Expanding	Interpret scientific results from illustrated text.	Keep logs or journals of features, events, or observations about the solar system.	Organize information about the body, following visually supported explanations.	Talk about the uses of natural phenomena, using pictures and illustrations.
Level 5, Bridging	Make inferences based on information found in classroom projects or science textbooks.	Explain characteristics of the solar system, using examples from events and observations.	Evaluate oral scenarios based on information about the body.	Examine relationships among natural phenomena.

Topics Grades 6–8	Body systems, organs	Weather, climate zones, natural disasters	Atoms, cells, molecules	Solar system
Language Domains	Reading	Writing	Listening	Speaking
Level 1, Starting	Match words or phrases to diagrams or models.	Draw and label charts of features, conditions, or occurrences, using newspapers or online resources.	Identify elements within models or diagrams, following oral directions.	Repeat definitions of key objects in the solar system with a partner.
Level 2, Emerging	Classify short descriptions of body systems using visual support.	Describe features, conditions, and occurrences around the world based on newspapers or online resources.	Match oral descriptions of functions of various elements with models or diagrams.	Describe the appearance and composition of objects in the solar system with a partner,.
Level 3, Developing	Find or sort visually supported information about processes (e.g., white cells versus red cells).	Compare features, conditions, and occurrences between two geographical areas based on information from multiple sources.	Arrange models or diagrams based on sequential oral directions.	Compare appearance and composition of objects in a galaxy with a partner.
Level 4, Expanding	Create sequenced steps to illustrate processes based on visually supported text.	Write a personal account describing the impact of features, conditions, or occurrences around the world, using multiple sources.	Reproduce models and diagrams based on visually supported materials.	Discuss or present illustrated processes involving planetary objects.
Level 5, Bridging	Make predictions from language-modified grade-level materials.	Interpret global impact of various features, conditions, or occurrences from language-modified grade-level material.	Design models or diagrams from texts without visual support.	Explain in technical vocabulary the structure of the universe using examples of planetary components.

Topics Grades 9–12	Scientific inquiry	Conservation	Nuclear functions	Compounds
Language Domains	Reading	Writing	Listening	Speaking
Level 1, Starting	Match vocabulary found in scientific inquiry with illustrated examples.	Label or list ways to protect the environment, using real-life examples or visuals.	Identify parts of elements from oral statements, using visuals or manipulatives.	Name common compounds from visual examples or symbols.
Level 2, Emerging	Categorize phrases and sentences found in scientific inquiry, using graphic support.	Describe ways to protect the environment, using graphic support.	Compare the arrangements of elements, using visual or graphic support, following oral statements.	Talk with a partner about changes involving chemical or physical reactions.
Level 3, Developing	Order paragraphs describing the process and product of scientific inquiry, using graphic support.	Compare results of experiments on ecology, using visual or graphic support.	Draw or build models of elements in small groups, following oral descriptions.	Outline with a partner the steps involved in chemical or physical reactions that result in the transformation of compounds.
Level 4, Expanding	Select relevant information related to the process and product of scientific inquiry, using graphic support.	Summarize experiments or research on ecology, using visual or graphic support.	Create representations of properties, characteristics, and uses in small groups, following oral descriptions.	Report information on processes and results of chemical or physical reactions, with a partner.
Level 5, Bridging	Analyze explanations and conclusions from scientific inquiry examples.	Select ecological methods and explain their applications.	Evaluate classmates' oral reports on the elements.	Explain changes in matter and their application to real-world situations.

Social Studies

Topics Grades Pre-K–K	School	Friends and family	Transportation	Home
Language Domains	Reading	Writing	Listening	Speaking
Level 1, Starting	Identify pictures of various places in the school in groups.	Draw pictures of a friend or shared experiences with a friend.	Match sounds of transportation vehicles with their pictures.	Identify names of different types of homes from pictures.
Level 2, Emerging	Match names of school workers with pictures from books or other sources.	Label pictures of self, friends, or family members, using letters or scribble writing.	Role-play or gesture in groups, based on transportation-themed songs or chants.	Practice songs or chants that describe homes, in large groups.
Level 3, Developing	Put in alphabetical order labeled pictures of classroom objects.	Draw familiar people and places, using pictures and letters, scribble writing, or invented spelling.	Role-play transportation scenes in groups, following oral directions.	Deliver predictable sentence patterns based on visuals about homes.
Level 4, Expanding	Identify capital letters, from a list of school worker names, with a partner.	Make illustrated lists of familiar people and places in pairs or small groups, using letters, words, and invented spelling.	Make different types of vehicles in teams or groups, following oral directions.	Compare different types of homes found in picture books.
Level 5, Bridging	Identify school-related vocabulary in illustrated phrases and sentences.	Create picture book or stories based on familiar people and places with a partner, using words, phrases, and invented spelling.	Identify types of transportation, following oral descriptions.	Talk about location of homes.

Topics Grades 1–3	History	Money	Maps	Cultural heritage
Language Domains	Reading	Writing	Listening	Speaking
Level 1, Starting	Arrange historical figures and events in chronological order, using visuals.	Label coins representing U.S. or other economies.	Point to or mark major map features, following oral commands.	Locate landmarks and people in pictures.
Level 2, Emerging	Label historical figures and events using visual and graphic support.	Draw or list ways in which people use money, in small groups.	Identify and point to physical features (on maps, globes), following oral commands.	Describe customs or traditions, using visual support.
Level 3, Developing	Sequence historical figures and events ,using graphic support.	Write about ways to earn, spend, and save money, in small groups.	Locate places or physical features, following oral directions.	Talk about cultural heritage with a partner, using artifacts.
Level 4, Expanding	Link historical figures, events, and ideas, using graphic support.	Explain in small groups how families around the world use money.	Compare and contrast physical features, following oral directions.	Compare aspects of cultural heritage, using visual support.
Level 5, Bridging	Explain how historical figures, events, and ideas have changed over time.	Evaluate how families and businesses need and use money.	Build models of physical features, following oral directions.	Report on cultural heritage information gathered from various sources.

Topics Grades 4–5	Contributions of people	Immigration	Prehistoric animals and artifacts	Topography
Language Domains	Reading	Writing	Listening	Speaking
Level 1, Starting	Match places and events to people, using visuals.	Match family members and historical figures with countries of origin, using maps or charts.	Identify prehistoric animals and artifacts in pictures, following oral descriptions.	State directions and locations with guidance from peers, using gestures or realia.
Level 2, Emerging	Combine cultures, traits, or contributions of people, using graphic organizers or illustrations.	Create family trees using photos and graphic organizers.	Match prehistoric animals and artifacts with their environments in videos, following oral descriptions.	Identify characteristics of places in small groups.
Level 3, Developing	Evaluate cultures, traits, or contributions of people, using graphic organizers or illustrations.	Put together illustrated family histories, using journals and diaries.	Put prehistoric animals and artifacts in chronological order on a timeline, following oral readings.	Locate and describe places, using realia, through interaction with peers.
Level 4, Expanding	Summarize information found in multiple illustrated sources about contributions of specific people.	Report on information based on interviews of family or historic journeys.	Role-play scenes from the past involving prehistoric animals and artifacts, following videos, movies, or oral readings.	Compare the location of places in groups, using realia and media.
Level 5, Bridging	Reach conclusions about contributions of specific people based on information collected from modified grade-level texts.	Write a paragraph about the causes and impact of immigration.	Role-play the role of anthropologists and paleontologists, following videos, movies, or oral readings.	Give presentations about places in groups, using visual support.

Topics Grades 6–8	U.S. history	Perspectives on people, places, and cultures	Latitude, longitude, maps	Freedom and democracy
Language Domains	Reading	Writing	Listening	Speaking
Level 1, Starting	Match descriptions of actions or events in U.S. history with photographs or other visuals.	List features of people, places, or time periods, using visuals.	Find locations with a partner, following oral directions.	Answer simple questions based on illustrated historical scenes.
Level 2, Emerging	Classify visually supported short text about actions or events in U.S. history.	Describe people, places, or periods, using visuals or realia.	Categorize features or locations on maps with a partner, following oral statements.	Make simple statements about illustrated historical scenes related to freedom and democracy.
Level 3, Developing	Order paragraphs describing actions or events in U.S. history, using visual and graphic support.	Compare features of people, places, or periods, using visuals or realia.	Identify features or locations on maps with a partner, following oral statements.	Describe or role-play historical scripts based on illustrations or other historical visuals related to freedom and democracy.
Level 4, Expanding	Match actions or events in U.S. history to summaries, using visual or graphic support.	Give examples of cross-cultural connections among features of people, places, or periods, using visuals or realia.	Match oral descriptions of features or locations on maps with a partner.	Take a position and give reasons for it, based on illustrations or other historical visuals related to freedom and democracy.
Level 5, Bridging	Identify and interpret relationships among actions or events in U.S. history, using information found in modified grade-level texts.	Define and provide support for cross-cultural perspectives.	Put detailed descriptions of features or locations in sequence, using oral travelogues.	Evaluate different hypothetical historical scenarios and describe their impact on the current situation.

Topics Grades 9–12	Global economy, supply and demand, money and banking	Cultural diversity and cohesion, international and multinational organizations	Supreme Court cases; federal, civil, and individual rights; social issues and inequities	Human populations
Language Domains	Reading	Writing	Listening	Speaking
Level 1, Starting	Connect areas on maps or globes and their products or monetary units, using visually supported sources.	Brainstorm in small groups and record examples of multicultural institutions or symbols.	Find basic information in illustrations and photographs after listening to oral statements,.	Exchange with a partner facts about peoples, languages, or cultures of local communities or native countries.
Level 2, Emerging	Gather information about places, products, or monetary units from newspapers, charts, or graphs.	List and define multicultural issues, symbols, or institutions in small groups.	Identify topics or political issues in illustrations and photographs after listening to oral descriptions.	Share personal experiences and reactions to migration or immigration with a partner.
Level 3, Developing	Identify trends in monetary values or production from charts, tables, or graphs.	Compare ideal and real situations for multicultural issues or organizations, using graphic organizers.	Compare oral summaries of political situations and visual representations.	Discuss demographic shifts, migration, immigration, languages, or cultures in small groups.
Level 4, Expanding	Predict future trends in monetary values or production from visually supported text.	State and defend a position on multicultural issues or organizations, using feedback from a partner.	Interpret peer reenactments or presentations based on political situations as seen in the media.	Explain the effect of demographic shifts or migration on peoples, languages, or cultures in small groups.
Level 5, Bridging	Interpret economic trends based on language-modified grade-level materials.	Write essays or poems that address or pose creative solutions to multicultural issues.	Evaluate mock trials or political speeches produced by classmates.	Present orally the characteristics, distribution, and migration of peoples, their languages, and their cultures.

Academic Vocabulary for Math, Science, and Social Studies

General Academic Vocabulary

The following general academic vocabulary list is adapted from the Academic Word List (AWL), developed by Averil Coxhead in 2000 and published in the 34th volume of *TESOL Quarterly*. The AWL consists of 570 word families that occur frequently in academic texts. An example of a word family is represented by the following list of words for the headword *distribute*:

distributed

distributing

distribution

distributional

distributions

distributive

distributor

distributors

redistribute

redistributed

redistributes

redistributing

redistribution

Because the AWL is not restricted to a specific field of study, it is very useful for ELLs in many academic settings. Content area teachers should use these words when they teach and create assessment instruments for ELLs. ELLs who are exposed to contexts requiring the AWL usage are likely to be able to master academic material with more confidence and efficiency.

The list below contains only the headwords for the AWL word families and is organized from the most frequent (1) to the least frequent (10) academic words.

1. analyze approach area assess assume authority available benefit concept consist context constitute contract data define derive distribute economy environment establish estimate evident factor finance formula function income indicate individual interpret involve issue labor legal legislate major method occur percent period principle proceed process policy require research respond role section sector significant similar source specific structure theory vary

2. achieve acquire administrate affect appropriate aspect assist category chapter commission community complex compute conclude conduct consequent construct consume credit culture design distinct equate element evaluate feature final focus impact injure institute invest item journal maintain normal obtain participate perceive positive potential previous primary purchase range region regulate relevant reside resource restrict secure seek select site strategy survey text tradition transfer

3. alternative circumstance comment compensate component consent considerable constant constrain contribute convene coordinate core corporate correspond criteria deduce demonstrate document dominate emphasis ensure exclude fund framework illustrate immigrate imply initial instance interact justify layer link locate maximize minor negate outcome partner philosophy physical proportion publish react register rely remove scheme sequence shift specify sufficient task technical technique technology valid volume

4. access adequacy annual apparent approximate attitude attribute civil code commit communicate concentrate confer contrast cycle debate despite dimension domestic emerge error ethnic goal grant hence hypothesis implement implicate impose integrate internal investigate job label mechanism obvious occupy option output overall parallel parameter phase predict prior principal professional project promote regime resolve retain series statistic status stress subsequent sum summary undertake

5. academy adjust alter amend aware capacity challenge clause compound conflict consult contact decline discrete draft enable energy enforce entity equivalent evolve expand expose external facilitate fundamental generate generation image liberal license logic margin mental medical modify monitor network notion objective orient perspective precise prime psychology pursue ratio reject revenue stable style substitute sustain symbol target transit trend version welfare whereas

6. abstract acknowledge accuracy aggregate allocate assign attach author bond brief capable cite cooperate discriminate display diverse domain edit enhance estate exceed expert explicit federal fee flexible furthermore gender ignorance incentive incorporate incidence index inhibit initiate input instruct intelligence interval lecture migrate minimum ministry motive neutral nevertheless overseas precede presume rational recover reveal scope subsidy tape trace transform transport underlie utilize

7. adapt adult advocate aid channel chemical classic comprehensive comprise confirm contrary convert couple decade definite deny differentiate dispose dynamic equip eliminate empirical extract file finite foundation globe grade guarantee hierarchy identical ideology infer innovate insert intervene isolate media mode paradigm phenomenon priority prohibit publication quote release reverse simulate sole somewhat submit successor survive thesis topic transmit ultimate unique visible voluntary

8. abandon accompany accumulate ambiguous appendix appreciate arbitrary automate bias chart clarify commodity complement conform contemporary contradict crucial currency denote detect deviate displace drama eventual exhibit exploit fluctuate guideline highlight implicit induce inevitable infrastructure inspect intense manipulate minimize nuclear offset paragraph plus practitioner predominant prospect radical random reinforce restore revise schedule tense terminate theme thereby uniform vehicle via virtual visual widespread

9. accommodate analogy anticipate assure attain behalf cease coherent coincide commence compatible concurrent confine controversy converse device devote diminish distort duration erode ethic found format inherent insight integral intermediate manual mature mediate medium military minimal mutual norm overlap passive portion preliminary protocol qualitative refine relax restrain revolution rigid route scenario sphere subordinate supplement suspend team temporary trigger unify violate vision

10. adjacent albeit assemble collapse colleague compile conceive convince depress encounter enormous forthcoming incline integrity intrinsic invoke levy likewise nonetheless notwithstanding odd ongoing panel persist pose reluctance so-called straightforward undergo whereby

Source: Coxhead, A. (2000). A new academic word list. *TESOL Quarterly, 34*, 213–238. The comprehensive AWL is available at www.victoria.ac.nz/lals/staff/Averil-Coxhead/awl/

Specific Academic Vocabulary for Math, Science, and Social Studies

Content area teachers need to be aware of the importance academic vocabulary plays in instruction and assessment. While the AWL presents academic vocabulary common to many disciplines, the vocabulary critical to the understanding of content area concepts taught in schools is given. Content area teachers should constantly incorporate these terms in their instruction and assessment of ELLs. Many programs that emphasize the teaching of high-frequency words to ELLs do not provide the background knowledge needed for student success. The systematic usage of the vocabulary lists described below will ensure content area assessments will primarily measure content knowledge, not language proficiency of ELLs.

The lists, based on the work of Marzano (2004) and the Tennessee Academic Vocabulary Project (www.rcs.k12.tn.us/rc/departments/ITS/Teacher_Resources/State_Department_WordList_Final.pdf) are organized by grade level and content area and are adapted from the work done by the staff of Illinois' U-46 School District, available at http://www.u-46.org/roadmap/dyncat.cfm?catid=246.

Pre-K

Math	Science	Social Studies
calendar	cold	**Civics**
big	color	rule
circle	different	school
first	grow	take turns
in	hot	**Economics**
last	same	job
less	scientist	money
little	tool	**Geography**
medium	**Health**	family
more	feelings	home
number	hand washing	neighborhood
on	healthy	weather
out	sick	**History**
rectangle	**Technology**	friend
square	computer	leader
triangle		role
under		

Kindergarten

Math	Science	Social Studies
Number Sense	**Earth/Science**	**Culture/Society**
number	change	community
same	color	family
different	day	school
Estimation/ Measurement	night	**Economics**
calendar	season	job
date	weather	money
day	**Life/Health**	**Geography**
graph	human body	farm
less than	feelings	ocean
measure	**Physical**	**Government**
month	float	flag
more than	large	rule
week	sink	
year	small	
Geometry	wood	
circle		
rectangle		
square		
triangle		
Algebra		
pattern		
opposite		
Data Analysis		
predict		
plus		
equal		

First Grade

Math	Science	Social Studies
Number Sense	**Scientific Inquiry**	**Culture/Society**
addition	observation	holiday
difference	label	relatives
equal	properties	respect
even/odd number	record	responsibility
greater than/less than	sort	**Economics**
subtraction	**Life/Earth**	needs/wants
sum	living/non-living	**Geography**
tallies	plant	city
Estimation/Measurement	**Physical**	direction
centimeter	liquid	east
coin	solid	globe
dime	mixture	map
dollar		north
inch		south
money		symbols
nickel		west
penny		**Government**
quarter		vote
temperature		
Geometry		
hexagon		
rhombus		
trapezoid		
Algebra		
pattern		
Data Analysis		
graph		

Second Grade

Math	Science	Social Studies
Number Sense	**Scientific Inquiry**	**Culture/Society**
addends	cause/effect	ancestors
decimal point	conclusion	**Economics**
diagram	experiment	goods
digit	hypothesis	resources
divide	life/health	services
	exercise	**Geography**
equivalent	habitat	cardinal directions
fraction	life cycle	compass rose
model	predator	continent
multiply	prey	geography
Estimation/Measurement	**Physical**	landform
Celsius	balance	map key
Fahrenheit	counterweight	country
foot	gravity	**Government**
meter	motion	capital
yard	rotate	citizen
Geometry	**Earth/Science**	election
perimeter	air	law
symmetry	cloud	leader
two/three dimensional	environment	**History**
Algebra	recycle	timeline
array	weather	tradition
Data Analysis		
data		
graph		
median		
range		

Third Grade

Math	Science	Social Studies
Number Sense	**Scientific Method**	**Culture/Society**
denominator	conclusion	culture
factor	experiment	immigration
numerator	hypothesis	choices
remainder	observation	majority
Estimation/Measurement	problem	minority
length	**Life / Health**	rights
volume	disease	**Economics**
width	habits	production
depth	health	products
Geometry	hygiene	profit
angle	nutrition	salary
base	wellness	wages
circumference	**Physical**	**Geography**
congruent	attract	atlas
diameter	battery	boundary
edge	circuit	country
face	conductor	equator
intersecting	electrical current	rural
parallelogram	electricity	state
polygon	insulator	suburban
vertex	invention	urban
Algebra	magnet	**Government**
ordered pair	repel	governor
Data Analysis	**Earth/Space**	local
check	evaporation	mayor
elapsed time	geology	national
probability	mineral	
solution	reflection	
strategy	rock	
	crystal	

Fourth Grade

Math	Science	Social Studies
Number Sense	**Life /Health**	**Culture/Society**
base-ten	adaptation	customs
billion	body structure	ethnicity
common denominator	function	heritage
coordinates	life forms	independence
decimals	**Physical**	nationality
dividend	condensation	slave
divisor	energy	**Economics**
exponents	evaporation	agriculture
hundreds	friction	capital resource
millions	heat	demand
quotient	mass	economy
Estimation/Measurement	precipitation	export
capacity	surface tension	human resource
fraction/improper fraction	vibration	import
mixed numbers	**Earth/Space**	manufacturing
Geometry	climate	natural resource
parallelogram	erosion	supply
perpendicular	fossil	tax
reflection/flip	(non)renewable resources	**Geography**
right angle	orbit	cardinal
rotation turn	planet	directions
translation slide	recycling	elevation
Algebra	solar system	geography
axis	star	hemisphere
common Factor		intermediate
formula		latitude
inequality		longitude
interval		population
Data Analysis		region
average		scale
mean		**Government**
median		branches of government
graph (line/circle/picto/bar)		citizenship
range		federal
mode		local
		state
		History
		immigration

Fifth Grade

Math	Science	Social Studies
Number Sense	**General Scientific**	**Culture/Society**
composite number	control	compromise
convert	validity	conflict
greatest common factor	variable	cooperation
least common multiple	**Health**	diverse
percent	body systems	Europeans
prime number	drug Abuse	Native Americans
scientific notation	mature	society
Algebra	peer pressure	tolerance
function	puberty	**Economics**
variable	social Pressure	free enterprise
Geometry	**Life**	trade
acute angle	carbon dioxide	**Geography**
adjacent	landfill	legend
equilateral triangle	oxygen	navigation
isosceles triangle	photosynthesis	**Government**
obtuse angle	pollination	Bill of Rights
radius	pollution	Constitution
reduced form	reproduction	Declaration of
scalene triangle	**Physical**	Independence
simplify	element	democracy
congruent	neutral	**History**
Data Analysis		colonization
mean		exploration
median		influences
mode		revolution
proportion		settlement
range		Civil War
ratio		

Sixth Grade

Math	Science	Social Studies
Number Sense	**Scientific Method**	**Culture/Society**
integer	control	architecture
inverse function	hypothesis	artisan
like terms	observation	caste
place value	scientific method	domesticate
reciprocal	system	guilds
square root	variable	hieroglyph
square number	**Life / Health**	legacy
standard notation	gene	monotheism
Estimation/Measurement	immunity	polytheism
accurate	sexual	religion
approximate	**Physical**	social class
Geometry	density	**Economics**
angle degree	dormant	currency
bisector	germinate	economy
congruent	acid	specialization
coordinates	base	surplus
geometric solids	pendulum	**Geography**
(ir)regular polygon	pressure	meridians
quadrant	velocity	parallels
Algebra	**Earth/Space**	**Government**
algebraic expression	absorb	acropolis
base	aquatic	aristocrat
exponent	biomes	dictator
significant	ecosystem	feudalism
Data Analysis	environment	monarchy
frequency	orientation	nobility
outcome	refract	republic
spreadsheet	spectrum	tyranny
statistics: mean, median, mode, range.	terrestrial	**History**
	fossil fuel	ancient
	radiation	artifact
		civilization
		descendant
		empire
		migration
		prehistory
		technology
		theory

Seventh Grade

Math	Science	Social Studies
Number Sense	**Scientific Inquiry**	**Culture**
exponent	analyzing	culture
prefix (bi, tri, quad.)	characteristic	diversity
proportion	classify	ethnicity
ratio	conclusion	immigration
rational number	dependent variable	literacy
Estimation/Measurement	independent variable	prejudice
area	interpret	racism
conversion	metric unit	refugee
dimensions	observation	urban/rural
perimeter	relationship	**Economics**
Geometry	**Life**	tax
congruent	abiotic /biotic	technology
similar	adaptation	debt
Algebra	biome	economics
equation	cells	globalization
evaluate	climate	poverty
properties	diversity	resources
sequence	ecosystem	**Geography**
simplify	heredity	climate
Data Analysis	organism	geography
probability	reproduction	landform
	species	**Government**
	Physical	citizenship
	density	genocide
	mass	government
	matter	
	volume	
	weight	

Eighth Grade

Math	Science	Social Studies
Number Sense	**Physical**	**History**
discount	acceleration	amend
interest	chemical reaction	appeal
tax	inertia	boycott
equivalent	friction	civil rights
(ir)rational numbers	force/strength	colony
Geometry	speed	compromise
transformation	velocity	constitution
surface area	work	democracy
circumference	compound	domestic/foreign
coordinate plane	element	executive/judicial/legislative branch
prism	period	federal
pyramid	bond	government
cylinder	motion	immigration
volume	mixture	national debt
Algebra	periodic	nationalism
distributive property	properties	representative
inequality	energy	republic
function	conservation	revolution
slope	atom	tariff
linear equation	molecule	tolerance
intercept	solution	treason
expression	**Earth**	
Pythagorean Theorem	radiation	
Data Analysis	seismic waves	
compound probability	plate tectonic	
	gravity	
	convection	
	atmosphere	
	solar system	
	weather	

Ninth to Twelfth Grade

Math

Number Sense	**Geometry**	**Algebra**
absolute value	arc	algebraic expressions
complex numbers	axis of symmetry	ascending
integers	central angle	coefficient
interest	chord	constant
(ir)rational number	congruent figures	coordinate plane
principal	conjecture	descending
scale factor	cosine	domain
rate of change	diagram	evaluate
Estimation/Measurement	line	function
conversion factor	pi	inequality
surface area	plane	intersecting lines
volume	postulate	intercept
Data Analysis and	proof	linear equation
Probability	radius	maximum/minimum of a
central tendency	ray	function
combination	reflection	polynomial
compound event	rotation	quadrant
probability	scale factor	radical expression
permutation	segment	range
	similar figures	reciprocal
	sine	root
	tangent	simplify
	theorem	substitute
	vertex	

Ninth to Twelfth Grade (*continued*)

Science		
Scientific Method	**Physical**	**Earth/Space**
analyze	bond	chemistry
characteristic	buoyancy/flotation	climate
classify	calorie	conduction
conclusion	chemical property/reaction	center/nucleus
control	circuit	crust
(in)dependent variables	constant	eclipse
experiment	current/flow	electromagnetic wave
hypothesis	density	electron
interpret	displacement	fission/fusion
observation	dynamics	galaxy
scientific method	balance	(in)organic
Life	force	layer
adaptation	frequency	mass
biological evolution	ion	matter
biology	isotope	movement
cellular cycle	magnitude	neutron
chromosome	mechanics	nucleus
DNA	metal	ozone
ecosystem	mol	precipitation
embryo	organic/inorganic	proton
environment	period	radiation
enzyme	physical property	radioactive disintegration
conservation	physics	universe
gene/ genome/	to precipitate	
habitat	pressure	
interdependence	radiation	
of organisms	reactant	
metabolism	reflection	
mutation	refraction	
natural selection	resistance	
organism	acceleration	
parasite	thermal	
photosynthesis	torsion	
protein	vector	
water cycle	wave	

Ninth to Twelfth Grade (*continued*)

Social Studies		
US History	**Economics**	**Civics**
affirmative action	annual percentage rate	bureaucracy
assimilation	assets	checks and Balances
capitalism	capital	citizen
communism	competition	civil liberties
demographics	consumer	Civil Rights
depression	corporation	democracy
feminism	credit	Democrat/Republican
foreign policy	debt	demographics
genocide	deficit	domestic policy
ideology	depression	due process
imperialism	economic systems	federalism
industrialization	economy	habeas corpus
nationalism	entrepreneur	ideology
nativism	factors of production	judicial review
neutrality	fiscal	Liberal /Conservative
propaganda	globalization	politics
radical	gross domestic product	sovereignty
segregation	incentive	referendum
socialism	inflation	representative
	investment	government (republic)
	liability	separation of powers
	market economy	
	monetary policy	
	mortgage	
	opportunity cost	
	recession	
	scarcity	
	supply and demand	
	tariff	

REFERENCES

Abedi, J., Courtney, M., & Leon, S. (2003). *Research-supported accommodations for English language learners in the NAEP* (CSE Tech. Rep. No. 586). Los Angeles: University of California's National Center for Research on Evaluation, Standards, and Student Testing.

Abedi, J., Courtney, M., Leon, S., Kao, J., & Azzam, T. (2006). *English language learners and math achievement: A study of opportunity to learn and language accommodation* (CSE Tech. Rep. No. 702). Los Angeles: University of California's National Center for Research on Evaluation, Standards, and Student Testing.

Abedi, J., Courtney, M., Mirocha, J., Leon, S., & Goldberg, J. (2005). *Language accommodations for English language learners in large-scale assessments: Bilingual dictionaries and linguistic modification* (CSE Tech. Rep. No. 666). Los Angeles: University of California's National Center for Research on Evaluation, Standards, and Student Testing.

Abedi, J., Hofstetter, C. H., Baker, E., & Lord, C. (2001). *NAEP math performance and test accommodations: Interactions with student language background* (CSE Tech. Rep. No. 536). Los Angeles: University of California's National Center for Research on Evaluation, Standards, and Student Testing.

Abedi, J., Hofstetter, C. H., & Lord, C. (2004). Assessment accommodations for English language learners: Implications for policy-based empirical research. *Review of Education Research, 74* (1), 1–28.

Abedi, J., Leon, S., & Mirocha, J. (2001, April). *Validity of standardized achievement tests for English language learners.* Paper presented at the annual meeting of the American Educational Research Association, Seattle, WA.

Abedi, J., & Lord, C. (2001). The language factor in mathematics tests. *Applied Measurement in Education, 14,* 219–234.

Abedi, J., Lord, C., Boscardin, C. K., & Miyoshi, J. (2001). *The effects of accommodations on the assessment of limited English proficient students in the National Assessment of Educational Progress* (Publication No. NCES 200113). Washington, DC: National Center for Educational Statistics.

Abedi, J., Lord, C., & Hofstetter, C. H. (1998). *Impact of selected background variables on students' NAEP mathematics performance* (CSE. Tech. Rep. No. 478). Los Angeles: University of California's National Center for Research on Evaluation, Standards, and Student Testing.

Abedi, J., Lord, C., & Plummer, J. R. (1997). *Final report on language background as available in NAEP mathematics performance* (CSE. Tech. Rep. No. 429). Los Angeles: University of California's National Center for Research on Evaluation, Standards, and Student Testing.

Abella, R., Urritia, J., & Shneyderman, A. (2005). An examination of the validity of English-language achievement test scores in an English language learner population. *Bilingual Research Journal, 29*(1), 127–144.

American Psychological Association. (1985). *Standards for educational and psychological testing.* Washington, DC: Author.

Anderson, R. S. (1998). *Why talk about different ways to grade? The shift from traditional assessment to alternative assessment: new direction for teaching and learning.* San Francisco: Jossey-Bass Publishers.

Anstrom, K. (1996, July). Defining the limited English proficient population. *Directions in Language and Education, 1*(9), 1–9.

Artiles, A. J., & Ortiz, A. A. (Eds.). (2002). *English language learners with special education needs: Identification, assessment, and instruction.* Washington, DC, and McHenry, IL: Center for Applied Linguistics and Delta Systems.

Bachman, L. F. (1990). *Fundamental considerations in language testing.* New York: Oxford University Press.

Baker, E.L., Aschbacher, P.R., Niemi, D., & Sato. E. (1992). *CRESST Performance assessment models: Assessing content area explanations.* Los Angeles: University of California's National Center for Research on Evaluation, Standards, and Student Testing.

Brown, H. D. (2004). *Language assessment: Principles and classroom practices.* Boston: Pearson.

Butler, F. A., & Stevens, R. (1997). *Accommodation strategies for English language learners on large-scale assessments: Student characteristics and other considerations* (CSE Tech. Rep. No. 448*).* Los Angeles: University of California's National Center for Research on Evaluation, Standards, and Student Testing.

Capps, R., Fix, M., Murray, J., Ost, J. Passel, J., & Herwantoro, S. (2006). *The new demography of American schools: Immigration and the No Child Left Behind Act.* Washington, DC: Urban Institute.

Castellon-Wellington, M. (2000). *The impact of preference for accommodations: The performance of ELLs on large-scale academic achievement tests* (CSE Tech. Rep. No. 524*).* Los Angeles: University of California's National Center for Research on Evaluation, Standards, and Student Testing.

Center for Universal Design. (1997). *The principles of universal design.* Retrieved July 20, 2007, from http://www.design.ncsu.edu/cud/about_ud/udprinciplestext.htm

Clarke, B., & Shinn, M. (2004). A preliminary investigation into the identification and development of early mathematics curriculum-based measurement. *School Psychology Review, 33*, 234–248.

Commission on Standards for School Mathematics. (1989). *Curriculum and evaluation standards for school mathematics.* Reston, VA: National Council of Teachers of Mathematics.

Commonwealth of Virginia Board of Education. (2002, November). *English language proficiency standards of learning for Virginia public schools.* Richmond, VA: Author.

Coombe, C., Folse, K., & Hubley, N. (2007). *A practical guide to assessing English language learners.* Ann Arbor: University of Michigan Press.

Crandall, J. (Ed.)(1985). *ESL through content-area instruction.* Englewood Cliffs, NJ: Prentice Hall Regents.

Croninger. B. (1991). *The social context of schooling: What research and theory can tell us.* Intercultural Development Research Association Newsletter, 18(5), 10–14.

Cummins, J. (1994). Knowledge, power and identity in teaching ESL. In F. Genesee (Ed.), *Educating second language children: The whole child, the whole curriculum, the whole community.* Cambridge, U.K.: Cambridge University Press.

Corasaniti Dale, T., & Cuevas, G.J. (1992). Integrating mathematics and language learning. In P.A. Richard-Amato & M.A. Snow (Eds.), *The multicultural classroom: Readings for content-area teachers.* White Plains, NY: Longman.

Danielson, C., & Abrutyn, L. (1997). *An introduction to using portfolios in the classroom.* Alexandria, VA: Association for Supervision and Curriculum Development.

Deno, S. L. (1992). The nature and development of curriculum-based measurement. *Preventing School Failure, 36*(2), 5–10.

Dolan, R. P., & Hall, T. E. (2001). Universal design for learning: Implications for large-scale assessment. *IDA Perspectives, 27* (4), 22–25.

Ernst-Slavit, G., Moore, M. & Maloney, C. (2002). Changing lives: Teaching English literature to ESL students. *Journal of Adolescent & Adult Literacy, 46*(2), 116–128.

Espinosa, L., & López, M.L. (2007). *Assessment Considerations for Young English Language Learners Across Different Levels of Accountability.* Commissioned paper for First 5 Los Angeles and the Pew Charitable Trusts' Early Childhood Accountability Project.

Figueroa, R. (1990). Assessment of linguistic minority group children. In C. Reynolds & R. Kamphaus (Eds.), *Handbook of psychological and educational assessment of children: Intelligence and achievement.* New York: The Guilford Press.

Figueroa, R. A., & Hernandez, S. (2000). *Testing Hispanic students in the United States: Technical and policy issues.* Washington, DC: President's Advisory Commission on Educational Excellence for Hispanic Americans.

Francis, D. J, Rivera, M., Lesaux, N., Kieffer, M., & Rivera, H. (2006). *Research-based recommendations for the use of accommodations in large-scale assessments.* Houston, TX: Center on Instruction.

Garcia, T., Paraent, L. R., Chen, L., Ferrara, S., Garavaglia, D., Johnson, E., Liang, J., Oppler, S., Searcy, C., Shieh, Y., & Ye, Y. (2000, November). *Study of a dual language test booklet in eighth grade mathematics: Final report.* Washington, DC: American Institutes for Research.

Garcia, G. E., & Pearson, P. D. (1994). Assessment and diversity. *Review of Research in Education, 20*, 337–391.

Genesee, F., & Upshur, J. A. (1996). *Classroom-based evaluation in second language education.* Cambridge, U.K.: Cambridge University Press.

Gomez, E. (1999, March). Creating large-scale assessment portfolios that include English language learners. *Perspectives on policy and practice.* Providence, RI: Northeast and Islands Regional Educational Laboratory.

Good. T. L. (1993). New direction in research on teacher and student expectations. *Midwestern Educational Researcher, 6*, 7–10, 17, 33.

Gottlieb, M. (2006). *Assessing English language learners: Bridges from language proficiency to academic achievement.* Thousand Oaks, CA: Corwin Press.

Grosvenor, L. (1993). *Student portfolios (Teacher to teacher).* Washington, DC: National Education Association Professional Library.

Hafner, A. L. (2000). *Evaluating the impact of test accommodations on test scores of LEP students and non-LEP students.* Dover: Delaware Department of Education.

Herman, J.L.,Aschbacher. P.R., & Winters, L.(1992). *A practical guide to alternative assessment.* Alexandria, VA: Association for Supervision and Curriculum Development.

Herrera, G. H., Murry, K. G., & Cabral, R. M. (2007). *Assessment accommodations for classroom teachers of culturally and linguistically diverse students.* Boston: Pearson.

Heubert, J., & Hauser, R. (Eds.). (1999). *High stakes testing for tracking, promotion and graduation.* Washington, DC: National Academy Press.

Hofstetter, C. H. (2003). Contextual and mathematics accommodation test effects for English language learners. *Applied Measurement in Education, 16*, 159–188.

Hosp, M., & Hosp, J. (2003). Curriculum-based measurement for reading, spelling, and math: How to do It and why. *Preventing School Failure, 48*(1), 10–17.

Hughes, A. (2003). *Testing for language teachers* (2nd ed.). Cambridge, U.K.: Cambridge University Press.

Kindler, A. (2002). *Survey of the states' limited English proficient students and available educational programs and services: 2000–2001 summary report.* Retrieved July 2, 2007, from http://www.ncela.gwu.edu/policy/states/reports/seareports/0001/sea0001.pdf

Kiplinger, V. L., Haug, C. A., & Abedi, J. (2000, June). *A math assessment should test math, not reading: One state's approach to the problem.* Paper presented at the 30th annual National Conference on Large-Scale Assessment, Snowbird, UT.

Koenig, J. A., & Bachman, L. F. (Eds.). (2004). *Keeping score for all: The effects of inclusion and accommodation policies on large-scale educational assessments*. Washington, DC: National Academies Press.

Krashen, S.D. (1985). *The input hypothesis: Issues and implications*. London: Longman.

Krashen, S.D., & Terrell, T.D. (1983). *The natural approach: Language acquisition in the classroom*. London: Prentice Hall Europe.

Lam, T. C. (1995). *Fairness in performance assessment*. Greensboro, NC: Eric Clearinghouse on Counseling and Student Services (ERIC Document Reproduction Service No. EDOCG9525).

Losardo, A., & Notari-Syverson, A. (2001). *Alternative approaches to assessing young children*. Baltimore, MD: Paul H. Brookes Publishing Company.

Macias, R. F. (1998). *Summary report of the survey of the states' limited English proficient students and available education programs and services, 1996–1997*. Washington, DC: National Clearinghouse for Bilingual Education.

Mahon, E. (2006). High-stakes testing and English language learners: Questions of validity. *Bilingual Research Journal, 30*(2), 479–97.

Maine Department of Education. (2002). *Methods used to identify K–12 students of limited English proficiency in Maine, 2001–2002*. Retrieved February 28, 2007, from http://www.maine.gov/education/esl

Marzano, R. J. (2004). *Building background knowledge for academic achievement: Research on what works in schools*. Alexandria, VA: Association for Supervision and Curriculum Development.

Menken, K. (2000). *What are the critical issues in wide-scale assessment of English language learners?* Retrieved on July 2, 2006 from http://www.ncela.gwu.edu/pubs/issuebriefs/ib6.htm

Mousavi, S. A. (2002). *An encyclopedic dictionary of language testing* (3rd ed.).Taipei, Taiwan: Tung Hua Books.

Moya, S., & O'Malley, M. (1994). A portfolio assessment model for ESL. *The Journal of Educational Issues of Language Minority Students, 13*, 13–36.

National Clearinghouse for English Language Acquisition (NCELA). (2007). *The growing number of limited English proficient Students*. Washington, DC: Author.

Niehoff, B., Turnley, W., & Yen, H. (2001). Exploring cultural differences in classroom expectations of students from the United States and Taiwan. *Journal of Education for Business, 76*(5), 289–93.

Nieto, S. (2004). *Affirming diversity: The sociopolitical context of multicultural education* (4th ed.). Boston: Pearson.

No Child Left Behind. (2001). Retrieved on August 15, 2006, from http://www.ed.gov/nclb/landing.jhtml

Nutta, J., & Pappamihiel, N. E. (2001, September). When something is lost in translation: The top five things mainstream content area teachers should know about English language learners. *Florida Educational Leadership,* pp. 35–38.

O'Malley, J.M. & Pierce, L.V. (1996). *Authentic assessment for English language learners: Practical approaches for teachers.* Menlo Park, CA: Addison-Wesley.

Pappamihiel, N. E., & Mihai, F. M. (2010). *Accommodations and English language learners: Inconsistencies in policies and practice.* Manuscript submitted for publication.

Pavri, S., & Fowler, S. (2005). Child find, screening, and tracking: Serving culturally and linguistically diverse children and families. *Appropriate screening, assessment, and family information gathering,* 3–22.

Peregoy, S. F., & Boyle, O. F. (2008). *Reading, writing, & learning in ESL: A resource book for K–12 teachers* (5th ed.). New York: Pearson.

Pierce, L. (2002). Performance-based assessment: Promoting achievement for English language learners. *ERIC/CLL News Bulletin,* 26(1), 1–3.

Ran, A. (2001). Traveling on parallel tracks: Chinese parents and English teachers. *Educational Research, 43,* 311–328.

Rhodes, R. L., Ochoa, S. H., & Ortiz, S. O. (2005). *Assessing culturally and linguistically diverse students: A practical guide.* Ney York: Guilford Press.

Rivera, C., & Stansfield, C. (2004). The effects of linguistic simplification of science test items on the performance of limited English proficient and monolingual English speaking students. *Educational Assessment, 9* (3–4), 79–105.

Scarcella, R. (1992). Providing culturally sensitive feedback. In P.A. Richard-Amato & M.A. Snow (Eds.), *The multicultural classroom: Readings for content area teachers.* Menlo Park, CA: Addison Wesley.

Scarcella, R. (2003). *Academic English: A conceptual framework* (Technical Report 2003-1). Santa Barbara: The University of California Linguistic Minority Research Institute.

Shaw, J. (1997). Threats to the validity of science performance assessments for English language learners. *Journal of Research in Science Teaching, 34,* 721–743.

Sireci, S.G., Li, S. & Scarpati, S. (2003). *The effects of test accommodation on test performance: A review of the literature.* Centre for Educational Assessment Research Report No. 485. Amherst: School of Education, University of Massachusetts.

Teachers of English to Speakers of Other Languages (TESOL). (2006). *Pre-K12 English language proficiency standards.* Alexandria, VA: Author.

Thernstrom, A., & Thernstrom, S. (2004). *No excuses. Closing the racial gap in learning.* New York: Simon and Schuster.

Thomas, W. P., & Collier, V. (1997). *School effectiveness for language minority students.* Washington, DC: National Clearinghouse for Bilingual Education.

U.S. Department of Education (2002*). Executive Summary. The No Child Left Behind Act of 2001*. Washington, DC: U.S. Government Printing Office.

Zehr, M.A. (2003). States developing tests for English language learners. *Education Week, 23*(13), 13–15.

Zehr, M.A. (2006). Scholars seek best ways to assess English-learners. *Education Week, 25*(18), 10.

INDEX

f after a page number indicates figure; t indicates table